# SIXTEEN
## AND
# COUNTING

# SIXTEEN AND COUNTING

### The National Championships of
## ALABAMA FOOTBALL

### Edited by KENNETH GADDY

The University of Alabama Press · Tuscaloosa

The University of Alabama Press
Tuscaloosa, Alabama 35487-0380
uapress.ua.edu

Published in cooperation with the Paul W. Bryant Museum.

Inquiries about reproducing material from this work should be addressed to the
University of Alabama Press.

Typeface: MinionPro

Cover image: Kenyon Drake caps off an exciting kickoff return with a touchdown dive,
photograph by Robert Sutton
Cover design: David Nees

Cataloging-in-Publication data is available from the Library of Congress.
ISBN: 978-0-8173-1969-4
E-ISBN: 978-0-8173-9164-5

"I'm here to see Johnny." That was a common refrain from visitors to the Paul W. Bryant Museum during John Mark Stallings' tenure on the museum's staff. Now that he is gone, I hope people can see a little bit of Johnny in each of us.

In Memory of John Mark Stallings

Our friend

# Contents

# CONTENTS

# Foreword

## BILL BATTLE

It is my pleasure to write the foreword to this book, which takes us in intimate detail through Alabama football national championships. It is the sequel to the book *Twelve and Counting* published in 2009. Hopefully another update will be required very soon.

Since early in its history, The University of Alabama's presidents have understood the value of successful athletics programs. They have supported the quest for excellence in athletics as well as in academics. That support has paid off in championship teams in football, gymnastics, softball, and men's and women's golf, which have created excitement, passion, and unity in the fan base. That passion has helped attract students from every state in the union and from seventy-seven foreign countries.

Winning national championships has been the goal of The University of Alabama football teams since the beginning. Athletics in general, and football in particular, are part of the DNA of The University of Alabama. Alabama led the south playing in Rose Bowl games in 1926, 1927, 1931, 1935, 1938, and 1946. In these six games Alabama won four, tied one, and lost one. In 1947 the Rose Bowl began its ties to the Big 10 and Pac 10.

Coaches who have won championships in football at Alabama are:

Wallace Wade: 1925, 1926, 1930
Frank Thomas: 1934, 1941

Paul Bryant: 1961, 1964, 1965, 1973, 1978, 1979
Gene Stallings: 1992
Nick Saban: 2009, 2011, 2012, 2015

It was my pleasure to play on Coach Bryant's first national championship team in 1961, and to be the teammate of Mal Moore, who served Alabama for forty-two years as an assistant coach, offensive coordinator, associate athletics director, and athletics director. It was also my pleasure to be coached by a young assistant coach out of Texas A&M University named Gene Stallings. It was easy to see, even at a young age, that Coach Stallings was destined for greatness both as a coach and a person.

Perhaps the greatest pleasure has been to serve as director of athletics over the last three years and watch Coach Saban reach an unprecedented level of success in modern day college football. Coach Saban and his teams have won four of the last seven national championships, and with a few plays turning out differently in two games, could have easily made it six of the last seven. We all hope Coach Saban enjoys many more years at The University of Alabama. And if he does, he will undoubtedly bring more championship trophies home to our University.

No one knows what the future will bring, but The University of Alabama is positioned very well to compete for championships in all sports and to educate and prepare our players to compete at the highest levels in life after graduation. That is our mission, and our coaches and administrative staff are committed to that cause.

There is great educational value in sports, especially team sports. I can assure you that Coach Saban—like Coach Bryant, Coach Stallings, and the others—has taught lessons that have prepared our players for life after graduation every bit as well as he has taught lessons that have prepared them to win championships.

It is my hope that you enjoy these stories of Alabama's national championships in football. I think you will find the stories to be very entertaining as they bring back fond memories of the players, coaches, and plays that made the difference in allowing Alabama to rise to the very top of the competitive college football playoff system. And I hope you remember that it really does take all of us to keep the Tide rising!

# SIXTEEN
### AND
# COUNTING

# Introduction

## Kenneth Gaddy

To understand the roots of Alabama football you need to only look to one person, William Gray Little. As a Sumter County boy exposed to "foot ball" during his boarding school days in Massachusetts he knew the sport would be a hit back home. Little became the father of Alabama football in 1892 as he introduced to campus the game that became the source of so much glory and acclaim. He envisioned the rough and tumble sport finding a home in the Deep South and the rest, as they say, is history.

The next milestone comes from a non-traditional source, not a coach or an athlete-but from a member of academia. The University of Alabama president George "Mike" Denny saw the new game as a recruiting tool not only to bring players to campus but *students* as well. His vision to make the Capstone a national household name is still paying dividends nearly a century later. Denny chose a battle-hardened veteran to put his plan into action. Wallace Wade had experience not only in the gridiron wars but also in real life warfare as a field artillery commander in World War I. (He later returned to this position in World War II.) Wade's "field general" demeanor became one of the standards by which all other coaches at Alabama are judged.

Lingering over the entire south in the 1920s were the physical and emotional scars of the Civil War and Reconstruction. Two landmark events helped heal a portion of the wounds. In the fall of 1922 Xen Scott led the team into the North to take on the University of Pennsylvania. That victory over the Quakers started a ripple that his successor, Wallace Wade, rode to greater glory three seasons later in the 1925 Rose Bowl.

On the firm foundation built by Little, Denny, Wade, and so many others, the coaching mantle was passed to Frank "Coach Tommy" Thomas in 1931. Coach Thomas not only built on the success of Wade but also did something special in response to an unusual turn of history. In 1943 The University of Alabama did not field a team. The call to duty in Europe and in the Pacific depleted the male student population on campus. He was able to reestablish the football program the next year using returning GIs and 4F players nicknamed the "War Babies." Another event in Thomas' tenure ripples through time to this day. Paul Bryant was recruited to play football for Alabama.

Paul Bryant took the reigns of the Tide at low ebb. He is famously quoted as saying "Mama called." The reason he returned to his alma mater has become a part of the tradition that is still embraced by the fans. Part of being "called" for a fan is being in the stands or by the radio when the Tide takes the field. Bryant concentrated on players, not plays. He later said he wanted to surround himself with people to whom football was important. That meant everyone from players to coaches to ticket takers. Bryant had a work ethic born in the Depression days in rural Arkansas. The hard work he demanded of his players soon bore the fruit our authors will illustrate.

One of Bryant's students, Gene Stallings, learned as a player and an assistant. Stallings quoted Sir Isaac Newton on the day he was announced as the twenty-second coach at Alabama, "If I can see farther than others it is because I am standing on the shoulders of giants." He had the advantage of the "giants" of Alabama football we recorded above and scores more.

Since our first edition of this book, *Twelve and Counting*, Coach Nick Saban has again thrust The University of Alabama to the top of the football world winning four more national titles with power-running games and dominating defenses. Mark Ingram and Derrick Henry earned Heisman trophies, adding new pages to the history books. Mal Moore's trip to Miami to "recruit" Saban may go down as one of the biggest milestones in Crimson Tide lore.

There have been over twenty-five hundred players in the history of Alabama football. Each one has "writ their name in Crimson flame" as the Bama fight song tells. From William Little to today's team they have given us, the fans, their all. The players are like fraternity brothers, even the ones who did not play together, no matter the number of decades that separate them. Wearing the crimson jersey is one of the highest badges of honor issued in the state.

From those attending the first game in 1892 (the crowd at the train station to meet the team returning from Pennsylvania), to the 102,000 that were packing Bryant-Denny Stadium, the fans have embraced the teams, the coaches, and the players. In the early days, newspapers and word of mouth were the only ways to follow the team. Later the ticker-tape parties in the larger cities in the state transformed into radio parties throughout the south. The growth of radio expanded the numbers and reach of the crimson nation. Today the Internet expands that reach worldwide. Fans have told us of walking through an airport and hearing "Roll Tide" and then remembering they are wearing a Bama shirt. Game days are a sea of crimson and white. The Bryant Museum has a database of over five hundred children named for Coach Bryant and has an annual Bryant namesake reunion.

The staff of the Paul W. Bryant Museum makes coming to work a pleasure. Their imprint is present throughout this book. Most of the writers benefited from their knowledge and the resources of the museum in their research. I also want to thank their families and mine for putting up with our long hours and even longer stories from the museum.

The staff of The University of Alabama Press have been great partners in this venture. Their hard work should not be overlooked.

So many people like Jeff Coleman, Hank Crisp, and Merrill Collins have contributed to the Alabama football legacy on and off the field. It seems inadequate to say a simple thank you, but I hope they know this attempt is heartfelt.

Finally, I would like to thank our distinguished lists of authors. Each one readily accepted the challenge to convey to you the story of a national championship year in a very limited number of words. We intentionally chose a different author for each championship season to give a unique voice to their accomplishments. Each championship team builds on the success of the teams before them, which led us to the *Sixteen and Counting* title.

On to the professional writers . . .

## CHAPTER ONE

# 1925

## ANDREW DOYLE

**H**istory is replete with legends that become less impressive under close scrutiny, and the sporting world is no exception. But it is difficult to overstate the achievements of Wallace Wade's 1925 Alabama team. Led by quarterback and defensive stalwart Pooley Hubert and sparked by the game-breaking ability of halfback Johnny Mack Brown, it dominated Southern Conference competition to win its second consecutive conference championship. A Rose Bowl invitation soon followed, but it came under inauspicious circumstances: Alabama was a fall-back choice only after several more heralded schools had turned down offers. Entering the game as a lightly regarded underdog and quickly falling behind by two touchdowns, the Tide faced a bitter finale to a brilliant season. But a miraculous come-from-behind victory shocked the so-called experts, sealed the national championship, and vaulted Alabama to football prominence.

This game rocked the football world—southern teams simply did not do things like this. During its early years southern football had been appallingly bad. American football evolved during the 1870s and 1880s at elite northeastern universities, especially Yale. But, plagued by two generations of endemic poverty following the Civil War and wary of Yankee cultural innovations, southerners showed no interest in football until a new generation began the slow process of integrating the South into the nation's economic

Coach Wallace Wade instructs his team at the 1925 Rose Bowl.

and cultural mainstream. The football fad spread among southern colleges between the late 1880s and mid-1890s, but enthusiasm hardly guarantees success. Virginia boldly took the South's best team northward in 1889, but it limped home after losing 72–0 to Penn and 115–0 to Princeton.

Southerners narrowed the sectional gap over the next three decades, but progress was excruciatingly slow. Southern states spent little on public education, and most, including Alabama, spent even less than they could afford. Virginia and Vanderbilt generally ranked as the best of the southern schools prior to World War I, and Sewanee was usually close behind. The Ivy Leaguers who invented football envisioned it as a pastime for the elite, and the prep schools from which Virginia, Vandy, and Sewanee recruited virtually all of their students generally had strong football programs.

(Public high schools were few in number, their football was usually second-rate, and the vast majority of southern boys worked full-time by age fifteen, anyway.) Virginia defeated mighty Yale in 1915, and Vandy tied them in 1910. But these were the best southern performances against the nation's leading teams prior to World War I. Alabama always lagged among the southern also-rans and did not tempt fate by venturing out of the region.

Bolstered by growing enrollments, greater revenues, and more public high schools from which to recruit, the public universities in the Deep South rose to prominence just before World War I. Georgia Tech was dominant in 1916 and 1917, and head coach John Heisman and his cheerleaders in the southern newspapers hailed the latter team as the first southern national champion. This claim is dubious at best. America entered World War I in March 1917, and the famed sports columnist Grantland Rice of the *New York Herald-Tribune* estimated that three-fourths of the nation's best football players had joined the armed services. Unlike the vast majority of their fellow coaches, Heisman and Pitt's Pop Warner persuaded their players to forego military service, and each cruised unbeaten through hapless competition. No poll system yet existed, but a majority of sportswriters nationwide chose Pitt as the best of an abysmally weak field. (Each team's roster had changed significantly, but Pitt defeated Tech in 1918, 1919, and 1920.)

Southern football improved dramatically during the early 1920s. While its overall quality remained well below that of the rest of the nation, the better southern teams occasionally won an intersectional game. Alabama pulled off one of these rare upsets with a shocking 9–7 victory over Penn in 1922. But that victory was a bright spot amid the usual mediocrity. Alabama promptly lost to Kentucky and finished with a 6–3–1 record. Head coach Xen Scott died after the season, and for the sixteenth time in its thirty-year football history, Alabama officials cast about for a new coach.

This time, they hit the jackpot. Thirty-one-year-old Wallace

Wade was a Tennessee native who had learned big-time football at Brown University, playing on the team that won the first Rose Bowl in 1916. As an assistant at Vanderbilt in 1921 and 1922, he oversaw the day-to-day management of the team while head coach Dan McGugin maintained a Nashville law practice. Part-time coaches were a throwback to an earlier era, but Wade was totally committed to his profession. His skill and dedication temporarily reversed Vanderbilt's decline, and it posted its last undefeated seasons while he worked there.

As he did with most issues facing the school, Alabama president George Denny made the final decision to hire Wade. Upon assuming office in 1914, Denny personally oversaw the football program. Financial support for athletes was the linchpin of any successful program, since outmoded rules originally conceived in Victorian England banned athletic scholarships. So like all but a handful of schools, Alabama provided under-the-table funding to cover tuition and living expenses. But unlike most of his peers, Denny personally supervised the process. And his micromanagement included attendance at many practices, at which he stood on the sideline puffing casually on his pipe. Friction quickly developed between Denny and the equally strong-willed Wade, and it was a factor in the latter's departure in 1931. But for the moment, the new coach focused on building his team.

The fundamentals of blocking and tackling became Wade's first order of business. While southern high school programs had increased in number and quality, most recruits remained raw. Daily practice for freshmen began in November, and the rest of the team joined them in February for rigorous spring drills. Stamina was crucial in that era, as a player who left the game could not return until the next quarter. Wade focused on the line, believing that winning in the trenches was essential to success. But he loved the wide-open offensive strategy of the 1920s, so Alabama ran a variety of reverses, flea-flickers, and misdirection plays. And he also loved the forward pass. It became legal in 1906, and a series of subsequent rule changes encouraged it, but few teams passed very often before 1917. The oval ball was difficult to grip, and most teams threw few passes unless opponents stymied their rushing attack. But by the 1920s, an increasing number of coaches fully integrated the pass into their offensive strategy. Wade was a leader in this trend, and Alabama was one of the nation's best passing teams by 1925.

When he took over in 1923, Wade recognized that he had a player with rare abilities. The Meridian, Mississippi, native Pooley Hubert was a bruising inside runner, strong lead blocker, and excellent passer. (He moved from fullback to quarterback in the middle of the 1925 season, but any back could throw the ball from the single-wing formation of that era.) Hubert was a devastating tackler with an uncanny ability to anticipate opponents' plays, and he played a rover position on defense. One of the few players who still eschewed a leather helmet, a bareheaded Hubert intimidated opponents prior to the snap by grimly pacing behind the defensive line. He also had rare leadership qualities. Professional coaches emerged in the 1890s and gradually gained control of college programs, but football insiders maintained the fiction that players' control of the game helped to build character. Thus, "coaching from the sidelines" during games remained against the rules. "Coach on the field" was more than a cliché then, and Hubert called offensive plays and defensive formations. Nicknamed "Papa" by his teammates, he became the cornerstone of the team.

The speed and moves of halfback Johnny Mack Brown complemented Hubert's power. Brown was a Dothan native described by one sportswriter as "slicker than an eel in a sea of stewed okra," and he became the big-play threat that Wade craved. As juniors in 1924, Hubert and Brown helped lead Alabama to its first-ever conference championship. (Known as the Southern Conference, it included eleven current SEC and seven current ACC schools among its twenty-two members.) But the Tide lost six key players to graduation, and pundits made Georgia Tech the favorite in 1925. Alabama's stellar backfield included Hubert, Brown, Emile "Red" Barnes, Grant Gillis, and Herschel Caldwell, but the line had a number of question marks.

The first two games revealed little about Alabama's true strength, since all major teams scheduled a couple of "warm-up games" against hopelessly overmatched opponents. The "Fighting Preachers" from Union College in Kentucky were the first designated victim, and Alabama romped to a 53–0 victory in Tuscaloosa. Next came Birmingham-Southern College, which the Tide dispatched 50–7. The Panthers' touchdown was the only surprise. Facing Alabama's reserves, they recovered a fumble and drove twenty-five yards for a touchdown. Only the most optimistic fan would have dared predict it, but Alabama surrendered no more points until the Rose Bowl.

LSU was the first of seven consecutive conference opponents. It had languished for decades below Alabama in the southern football hierarchy, but school officials hired the longtime Auburn coach Mike Donahue in 1923 and unveiled a beautiful new stadium the following year. Donahue stubbornly adhered to the ultraconservative "Yale system" he had learned as a player there, and restive alumni had shoved him out of Auburn for resisting current offensive trends. But the law of unintended consequences struck both programs: Auburn descended into the depths of southern football, from which it did not emerge until the 1950s. And LSU under Donahue never caught a whiff of greatness. LSU officials also displayed poor judgment by scheduling Alabama as their 1925 homecoming opponent. Seeing significant action for the first time, the Tide starters put on a show that horrified LSU alumni. Brown and halfback Hershel Caldwell ran to the outside virtually at will, and Hubert's inside rushing produced four touchdowns. The Tide racked up twenty-five first downs and 42 points. And if it's possible, the defense was even better: it not only shut out LSU, it held them without a single first down.

Next up came Sewanee, which in the topsy-turvy world of prewar southern football had once owned Alabama. But the "Sewanee jinx" ended when the Wade era began, and Alabama overwhelmed them 27–0 at Birmingham's Rickwood Field. For the second consecutive week, the crushing defense held a conference opponent without a first down. And the passing game was spectacular, completing nine of sixteen for 171 yards.

The Tide faced its toughest challenge on October 24, when it traveled to Atlanta to face Georgia Tech. Like virtually every other southern school, Alabama annually conceded home field advantage to Tech in exchange for greater revenue. The Atlanta market was the South's largest, as was Grant Field. The special train from Tuscaloosa to Atlanta included a record eight Pullman sleeper cars and several passenger cars. But in a practice nearly as old as southern football, the more adventurous students, many fueled by bootleg liquor, opted to clamber aboard an Atlanta-bound freight train.

Grant Field may have been the finest in the South, but advanced groundskeeping practices lay many decades away. Playing fields steadily deteriorated through the course of a season, and rain on game day inevitably created a quagmire. Neither offense moved the ball well; Tech gained only 125 yards and held Alabama under 100. Playing for field position and seeking to capitalize on a mistake, the teams often punted on second or third down. Undeterred by the mud, Johnny Mack Brown upended this strategy. Fielding a punt at his own 45, he followed a block by Red Barnes that took out three Tech defenders and sprinted untouched to the end zone. A tenacious Alabama defense held on to preserve the 7–0 victory. Brown provided the only scoring, but Wade and the sportswriters reserved their highest praise for Hubert's defensive play. He made or assisted in eighteen of Alabama's first twenty tackles and was instrumental in stopping Tech's inside rushing attack. Hubert later admitted that by the fourth quarter, "When I would hit the ground, I didn't know whether I was ever going to get to my feet again." But he had never left a game due to injury or fatigue, and he somehow managed to play the entire sixty minutes.

With several players nursing injuries after the battle with Tech, a flat Tide fought off a surprisingly strong Mississippi A&M (now Mississippi State) in its homecoming game. Facing a cold rain and a muddy field and not expecting a close game, Wade rested most of his starters during the first quarter. Fortunately for Alabama, Hubert played the entire game. In the first quarter, he tossed a fourteen-yard touchdown pass to end Wu Winslett that put Alabama up 6–0. Once again, a lone touchdown was the sum of the scoring. Playing most of the second half in its own territory, the defense preserved another shutout.

Wade worked the team unmercifully after their poor homecoming performance. Almost welcoming the break from practice, the Tide exploited its advantage in team speed in a 31–0 victory over Kentucky at Rickwood Field. Brown thrilled spectators with his "crow-hop" move on a seventy-nine-yard touchdown run, and he added another on a double reverse. Red Barnes returned a fumble seventy-five yards for a score, and Hubert added a final touchdown plunge. Joined by tackles Pete Camp and "Cupid" Perry, Hubert led the usual defensive dominance. Halfback Grant Gillis doubled as punter, and his booming kicks awed the crowd and pinned Kentucky in its own territory.

Alabama next met Florida in Montgomery. The Cramton Bowl was only one-third the size of Grant Field, but three years earlier it had joined the growing list of modern stadiums built during the economic boom of the 1920s. The "Alligators" had defeated Alabama in their only two previous games, including a season-ending heartbreaker in 1923 that had denied Wade a conference championship in his rookie season. But the Tide toyed with a Florida lineup that included three all-conference starters. Johnny Mack Brown caught two touchdown passes in the first half, and Red Barnes added two more on the ground in the second in a 34–0 victory.

In a tradition as old as college football, teams usually scheduled their leading rival in a Thanksgiving Day showdown. But Alabama and Auburn did not meet between 1907 and 1948, so Georgia filled that role in 1925. A victory would seal the Tide's second consecutive undefeated season and conference title, and Wade intensified his grueling practice routine. The game, however, proved anticlimactic. Georgia had a poor team that season, and Alabama's 27–0 victory surprised no one. Still smarting after Caldwell had replaced him in the starting lineup against Florida, Grant Gillis led a balanced Tide attack. He rushed for a team-leading fifty-four yards and also caught a fifty-yard touchdown pass from Winslett. And in a display of power that Bama fans never tired of, Hubert's inside rushing produced three touchdowns.

Alabama once again stood atop southern football, and individual honors poured in. A panel of game officials named Hubert the MVP of the Southern Conference, and Johnny Mack Brown and guard Bill Buckler joined him as starters on the all-conference team. Nearly every other starter ended up on somebody's second or third team. The *Atlanta Journal* columnist Morgan Blake gave unaccustomed praise to Alabama. He hailed Wade's brilliance, observing that neither Georgia nor Georgia Tech had scored on Alabama in six games over three years. And he declared Hubert a "Napoleon in football intellect." Grantland Rice topped the tributes by naming Hubert a second-team All-American, making him one of the few southern players ever to receive such an honor.

The Rose Bowl, however, remained an elusive dream. The nation's only bowl game until 1935, it pitted the Pacific Coast champion against the strongest team from the Northeast or Midwest. Bowl officials had never seriously considered a southern team, let alone invited one. But Alabama's unprecedented opportunity came after the University of Illinois halfback Red Grange ignited a ruckus by joining the Chicago Bears only hours after he had played his final college game. College football had been a big business for four decades, but a horde of self-righteous critics that included his own coach castigated Grange for violating football's "amateur purity." Worse, the fledgling NFL had a seedy image; it had an ethnic working-class fan base, owners with underworld ties, and franchises that regularly bankrupted or skipped town. Many university officials feared a public relations nightmare if they accepted a Rose Bowl bid—and cashed the fat check that came with it. West Coast champion Washington consequently dithered for a week before accepting a bid, and Dartmouth, Colgate, Princeton, and Michigan reportedly rejected invitations. George Denny, however, was not about to turn down this unprecedented opportunity.

A special train carrying the team, coaches, school officials, and a handful of fans departed Tuscaloosa on Saturday evening, December 19. Sixty-six hours later, Wade politely brushed off local dignitaries eager to show the team the wonders of southern California. This was no pleasure trip. He begrudged the players a couple of sightseeing jaunts, and he reversed an earlier decision by allowing the hotel manager to throw them a small Christmas celebration. Otherwise, they all remained focused. Bowl officials generously allowed them to practice at the Rose Bowl, allowing the Tide to get accustomed to a stadium that was much larger than any in the South. Wade held a light workout on Christmas Day, demanded ferocious scrimmages the next five days, and eased up only on New Year's Eve.

Southern Cal fans who disliked the Huskies dominated the Rose Bowl crowd, and they cheered as Alabama took the field. At the same time, anxious Alabamians crowded movie theaters, frater-

nal lodges, and roped-off streets for play-by-play telegraph updates
displayed on a graphic mock-up of a football field. Their spirits
faded when a nervous Tide looked nothing like the team that had
demolished southern competition. Led by the slashing runs and
bullet passes of star quarterback George Wilson, Washington
mounted an early seventy-yard touchdown drive. A flailing Alabama defense seemingly had forgotten how to tackle. Early in the
second quarter, Wilson shook off three Alabama defenders in the
process of ripping off a thirty-six-yard run to the Alabama twenty.
On the next play, he fired a twenty-yard touchdown pass. Extra
point attempts were not the automatics that bore today's fans, but
the second consecutive missed attempt seemed trivial. This was
turning into a blowout. Alabamians and the countless other southerners who cheered for their erstwhile rival worried helplessly.
Maybe the smug Yankees who dismissed southern football had
been right all along.

Sportswriters from around the nation shared opinions at halftime, and none believed Alabama had a prayer. Johnny Mack
Brown had shown flashes of brilliance, but they grumbled that the
pundits who made Hubert an All-American had been delusional.
But a headline in the *Los Angeles Examiner* summed up his performance: "Hubert Started Late, But Once He Was Off—WOW." Expecting a desperate Tide to pass, Washington dropped an extra defender into coverage. Also, Wilson was on the bench with injured
ribs, so their secondary lacked his run-stopping ability. Hubert exploited the opportunity by calling five consecutive quarterback
keepers. Following the blocking of center "Sherlock" Holmes and
guard Bruce Jones, his rushing accounted for all forty-two yards of
a touchdown drive. Bill Buckler kicked the extra point, and Alabama was back in the game.

Red Barnes opened the Tide's next possession with two strong
runs that brought the ball to the Alabama thirty-nine. Washington
then reverted to a seven-man front, so Hubert called a deep pass by

Grant Gillis. Although he was the starting quarterback for two seasons, Gillis had been eclipsed in 1925 by backfield mates Hubert, Brown, and Barnes, and he now fought for playing time. He more than redeemed himself by lofting a beautiful arcing pass that hit a speeding Brown in stride for a touchdown. Buckler was once again true, and Alabama led 14–12. The dazed Huskies attempted to regroup on the following possession, but they fumbled instead. On the first offensive snap, Hubert tossed a thirty-yard touchdown pass to Brown. The extra point failed, but Alabama led 20–12.

Alabama kept up the offensive pressure to start the fourth quarter, but the Huskies held them on fourth and goal at the one. Wilson then returned to the game, and his rushing spearheaded a drive that he capped with a twenty-seven-yard touchdown pass. Alabama's lead had dwindled to a single point, but Wilson could muster no more magic. Gillis intercepted one of his passes with six minutes left, and Herschel Caldwell picked off another one to end Washington's last-gasp drive.

The crowds gathered across Alabama exploded in frenzy when "Alabama Wins" flashed over the wire. Pandemonium reigned in Montgomery's Court Square, and fans triumphantly marched by torchlight through the downtown streets. Newspapers across the South—even the ultra-partisan journalists in Atlanta—proclaimed that the victory belonged to all southerners. The *Atlanta Georgian* proudly announced that the score should read, "The South 20, the West 19." Beneath the headline "Dixie Acclaims Her Heroes," the Atlanta *Journal* asserted, "All southern hearts are happy today over the outcome." The *Birmingham Age-Herald* generously shared Alabama's glory, declaring in a front-page editorial that it was "an impressive victory for the entire South."

A jubilant crowd in New Orleans hailed the Tide on its return trip, and Tuscaloosa resembled ancient Rome when the legions returned from a war of conquest. Freshmen pulled decorated wagons holding the players through streets thronged with cheering citizens. Those streets were so crowded that the caravan took an hour to cover the three-quarter-mile route from the train station to downtown. Governor Bill Brandon was among the dignitaries who greeted the heroes, and speakers praised them for improving the national image of Alabama and the South. A local attorney and civic leader tweaked the Yankees by proclaiming, "When the band plays 'Dixie' over the team, it can whip eleven Red Granges."

White southerners for whom the bitter wounds of the Civil War had not fully healed unquestionably saw this as a vindication of sectional pride. But southerners originally adopted football as a means of seeking greater inclusion in the nation their fathers had fought so hard to leave. And the success of the Crimson Tide was only possible in a modern industrial society that was becoming more like the North with each passing year. The social and cultural significance of this team should not be ignored, but neither should the young men who made it possible. Led by a brilliant coach not much older than his players, an inspired team dominated their southern peers and then pulled off one of the most shocking upsets in football history. Three-quarters of a century has inevitably eroded the historical memory of their achievements, but every contemporary fan who examines them afresh should come away impressed.

## TABLE 1

### 1925

Coach Wallace Wade

National Champions, Southern Conference Champions

Won 10, Lost 0

| Alabama | Opponent | | Location | Date |
|---|---|---|---|---|
| 53 | Union College | 0 | Tuscaloosa | Sept. 26 |
| 50 | B'ham Southern | 7 | Tuscaloosa | Oct. 2 |
| 42 | LSU | 0 | Baton Rouge | Oct. 10 |
| 27 | Sewanee | 0 | Birmingham | Oct. 17 |
| 7 | Georgia Tech | 0 | Atlanta | Oct. 24 |
| 6 | Miss. State | 0 | Tuscaloosa | Oct. 31 |
| 31 | Kentucky | 0 | Birmingham | Nov. 7 |
| 34 | Florida | 0 | Montgomery | Nov. 14 |
| 27 | Georgia | 0 | Birmingham | Nov. 26 |
| 20 | Washington | 19 | Rose Bowl | Jan. 21, 1926 |
| 297 | | 26 | | |

## CHAPTER TWO

# 1926

## TAYLOR WATSON

The tradition started here.

The University of Alabama president Dr. George W. Denny looked out of the train window as it pulled into the Tuscaloosa station on a cold November evening in 1922. It was not the train station's architecture he marveled at. It was the thousands of screaming University of Alabama football fans surrounding the station that amazed him on that Sunday afternoon. Dr. Denny and The University of Alabama football team were on their way back from a victorious Saturday against one of the nation's best teams, the University of Pennsylvania.

The tradition started here.

Dr. Denny smiled gleefully as he watched another mass of screaming Alabama fans surround the Tuscaloosa train station. These fans were celebrating another Bama victory and her first Southern Conference title in 1924.

The tradition started here.

President George W. Denny sat in the folding chair on top of the Capstone library steps, looking out over the thousands of cheering Alabama fans celebrating the Tide's great 1926 Rose Bowl victory over Washington and their crowning as 1925 national champions.

The tradition started here.

But if the tradition started here, could it be continued? Or was

Rough-and-tumble practices lead to game-day victories for the 1926 Tide.

it a fluke? With this recap of the 1926 season and the 1927 Rose Bowl game, I hope to show why this Crimson Tide team deserves to be the 1926 national champions, thus securing The University of Alabama's place in college football lore. A few sports historians, many fans from other schools, and some journalists have over the years refuted this national championship claim. So let me ask a question:

If not Alabama, who?

What other schools were undefeated in 1926?

If not Alabama, then who?

To help answer that question I am going to recount not only Alabama's season, but we are also going to look at the rest of the nation week by week.

So let's start with a little preseason hype!

Upon starting the 1926 season, several teams were expected to shine. I have listed the major powers for the 1926 season below:

In the Northeast:
Army
Brown
Boston College
Cornell
Dartmouth
Navy
Penn

In the Midwest:
Michigan
Notre Dame
Ohio State
Northwestern

On the West Coast:
Oregon State
Stanford
USC
Washington

In the southland:
Alabama
Tennessee
Vanderbilt
SMU
Georgia Tech

The schools listed above were just a few from hundreds of colleges that were playing football in 1926. By my estimation there were 72 schools playing "big" classification football and anywhere from 100 to 150 playing "small" classification.[1]

## THE 1926 SEASON

### Alabama vs. Vanderbilt

Alabama started the season a week earlier with a warm-up game against a tiny school from Jackson, Mississippi, Millsap College, winning 55–0. With October rolling around, Alabama's first conference contest would be an exciting game in Nashville. The team traveled by train to take on the Commodores of Vanderbilt. Expectations were so high in Nashville for the Alabama game that the Vanderbilt Athletic Association offered preseason tickets for the first time. Ticket sales did not disappoint with a record crowd of 20,000 to watch as Wallace Wade, a former assistant under Vanderbilt's Dan McGugin, would defeat his old master with a solid ground attack: Alabama 19, Vanderbilt 7.

### The Rest of the Nation

Most of the nation's top teams had no real problems with their first game of the season. Vanderbilt was the only major school to drop out of the perfect column during week 2.

### Alabama vs. Mississippi State

For the second week in a row, the Tide would be on the road. Alabama traveled to the Queen City of Meridian, Mississippi, to face a tough team from Starkville and play in front of another record crowd.

Alabama would leave with what would seem like an easy 26 to 7 victory, but the Bulldogs of State kept the game closer than the score indicated.

### The Rest of the Nation

By week 3, the season was in full swing, and of the seventy-two major schools, twenty-eight were still undefeated. There were no major upsets. In the Southern Conference, Tennessee had to rally late to defeat LSU in Baton Rouge. In the Big Ten, Michigan would crush cross-state rival Michigan State 55–3.

### Alabama vs. Georgia Tech

Alabama traveled east to Atlanta to take on Georgia Tech; even with a loss to start the season Georgia Tech was favored to beat Alabama by the Atlanta sportswriters. Turned out the sportswriters were wrong *as Alabama* held the Yellow Jackets to only two first downs the entire game. Alabama whitewashed Tech, 21–0, to stay undefeated and atop the Southern Conference.

### The Rest of the Nation

As the weather began to turn colder, the football season was beginning to heat up. SMU dropped out of the perfect column when the Missouri Tigers held them to a 7–7 tie. The Tigers from the plains would be unfortunate as well, having been defeated by the Tigers of LSU, 10–0. As the last game was played Saturday, only twenty-five teams still had zeros on the right side of the ledger.

### Alabama vs. Sewanee

The mighty Purple Tigers of Sewanee managed to do something that had not happened since the 1924 game against Centre College, they kept Bama out of the end zone. However, unlike the '24 game, Alabama managed a victory.

Sewanee's eleven played tough attacking defense and kept the game scoreless through three quarters. Early in the fourth period, Sewanee's captain Jack Todd was back to punt, when starting right tackle "Freddie" Prichard broke through the line and blocked the punt, both teams clamored for the ball, with Bama's Gordon Holmes reaching without success, as the ball bounced out of the end zone for a safety. That is 2 points for the good guys! Moreover, that is all it would take to win this Rickwood Field brawl.

## The Rest of the Nation

With the meat of the schedules starting all across the nation, two undefeated teams from the Midwest would meet in Evanston, Illinois. Northwestern dropped out of the perfect column with a heartbreaking loss to Notre Dame, 6–0. On the west coast, Washington State would defeat their in-state rival, the University of Washington, dropping the Huskies from the ranks of the perfect. Northwestern and Washington were not the only schools to lose during week 5; the race for the top was now down to nineteen.

## Alabama vs. LSU

Alabama's homecoming game started slow with both teams exchanging punts most of the first half, the only score coming on a seventeen-yard field goal by Alabama's Herschel "Rosy" Caldwell, giving Bama a 3–0 and that's all Bama would need, but the Tide added a couple of special teams touchdowns and an offensive score, to beat LSU 24–0.

## The Rest of the Nation

With only one day remaining in October, the nation's roster of perfect teams was getting shorter. The biggest upset of the day was the Wolverines of Ann Arbor losing at home to Navy 10–0. While Stanford remained undefeated after a 13–12 victory over USC, the Trojans were tagged with their first loss.

Illinois, with one loss, played old school football for a 3–0 win over Penn, while previously undefeated Cornell was upset 17–9 by a 5–1 Columbia team.

## Alabama vs. Kentucky

Alabama started November with a 14–0 win over Kentucky, taking the Tide to 7–0 and putting them a step closer to their third Southern Conference championship in a row.

## The Rest of the Nation

With only a month of football left, ten teams were still carrying zeros in the two right columns: Navy, Ohio State, Oregon State, Brown, the University of Tennessee, Notre Dame, Boston College, Army, Stanford, and Alabama.

## Alabama vs. Florida

Wallace Wade and the Crimson Tide traveled to Montgomery to play the Florida Gators in the state's largest football stadium, the Cramton Bowl. The packed house watched the Tide score one touchdown in the first quarter and two more in each of the remaining three quarters as Bama stampeded the Gators 49–0.

## The Rest of the Nation

During the eighth week of the regular season, five teams fell from the top.

Ohio State, in front of 90,000 fans, lost 17–16 to inter-state rival Michigan.

Southern Cal, 6–1, defeated Oregon State 17–7, leaving Stanford atop the Pac-Ten.

Tennessee lost to Vanderbilt, leaving Alabama as the only untied and undefeated team in the Southern Conference.

In the Bronx, two undefeated teams squared off when Notre Dame and the Cadets of Army took to the field. The game was tough until the middle of the third quarter when Notre Dame's back, Harry O' Boyle, handed to Cristy Flanagan and he ran untouched for a sixty-two-yard touchdown. The final score read Notre Dame 7, Army 0.

Later that day, Boston College remained undefeated but not perfect with a 21–21 game against Haskell Institute.

Then there were five: Stanford, Navy, Notre Dame, Brown, and Alabama.

## Alabama vs. Georgia

The week after the Florida game, University of Alabama officials received an offer to play in the 1927 Rose Bowl. Alabama officials would not confirm the game until after the December 5 Southern Intercollegiate Conference meeting, because the conference committee had to approved postseason play.

With all the talk of another Rose Bowl trip for the Tide, Wade was worried they might forget about the Thanksgiving Day game against the 5–3 Georgia Bulldogs. Georgia, which was on a two-game winning streak, had no power to stop Alabama's passing attack. Alabama won her ninth game of the season, 33–6. For the third straight year, Alabama was the Southern Conference champion.

## The Rest of the Nation

With Alabama and Stanford finished at 9–0, there were three other undefeated, untied teams getting ready for Saturday games. First was the 9–0 Brown University Bears versus Colgate. What should have been an easy win for the Bears of Providence turned into a disaster when the 5–2–1 Raiders tied the game at 10 and held on to the finish, thus giving Brown its only blow of the year.

Then there were four.

Next up was the undefeated Fighting Irish. The Irish traveled to Pittsburgh to take on Carnegie Tech. Notre Dame and her head coach were so confident after their Army victory that Coach Rockne went to Chicago to watch the Army/Navy game instead of traveling to Pittsburgh with his team. It turned out to be a good choice because he saw a better game in Chicago! Notre Dame's game wasn't even close. The tiny school, started by the industrialist and philanthropist Andrew Carnegie in 1900, blanked the mighty Irish 19–0 in arguably the biggest upset in college football history and certainly one of the biggest blunders by a head coach.

And then there were three.

Next up was once-beaten Army versus 9–0 Navy. The Corps of Cadets and the Regiment of Midshipmen fought to a 14–14 half-time score. Army scored first in the second half, making it 21–14. With the clock winding down, Navy moved the ball down the field and scored on a reverse play. With the extra point, the game was tied 21–21. Navy joined Army with a mark on the right side of the ledger.

In three months, 15 million fans had watched a great number of college football games while millions more listened over the airways.

By this time, only two undefeated teams remained: Alabama and Stanford.

As was the case in 1925, the 1926 Crimson Tide received no respect from outside the South. Jack James, writing for the International News Service about the upcoming Rose Bowl game, stated, "Alabama must be superhuman to gain victory."

Los Angeles reporter Jim Reynolds said: "Stanford had no parallel in (west) coast history."

Thankfully for Alabama fans, the football "experts" were not playing the game.

## THE POSTSEASON

### The 1927 Rose Bowl: Alabama vs. Stanford

The 1927 Rose Bowl was drawing so much attention that NBC radio decided to broadcast the game, making it the first football game broadcast nationwide.

Alabama would begin the game without starting center Gordon Holmes, who also was a defensive juggernaut. Also out for the game was halfback James Johnson. On the first play from scrimmage, Stanford's fullback and main passer, Clifford Hoffman, chunked the ball forty yards down field to right end Ted Shipkey for a first down on Bama's twenty-seven yard line. The Alabama defense held and Stanford missed a field goal attempt. The Tide ran three straight running plays, but failed to gain a first down, and "Red" Barnes punted deep to Stanford's William Hyland. The instant that Hyland caught the ball Bama's mighty Fred Pickhard was right there with a hit! Loose ball! Fumble! Herschel Caldwell was Johnny-on-the-spot, and he had a clear line straight into the end zone for 6, but he drops the ball. Stanford's Shipkey falls on it. It's now first and ten, Stanford, after a key opportunity was blown by Bama.

The teams traded punts until late in the first quarter when Stanford drove the ball sixty-three yards with a brilliant mix of passes, fake reverses, and runs to push into the end zone as the clock reached zero.

The score after one quarter of play: Stanford 7, Alabama 0.

Defense was the name of the game for the second quarter, with Stanford out-gaining Alabama in total yardage but no change to the scoreboard for either team. The first half ended with the score Stanford 7, Alabama 0.

What a defensive struggle, what a game!

The third quarter was just like the first two, but Stanford players were slowing some from all the ferocious hits they were absorbing from the southern boys. The fourth quarter started with both teams exchanging punts. After a three-and-out, Stanford's Hoffmann launched a rainmaker of a punt, all the way back to Bama's twenty, where Archie Taylor was waiting—fumble!

Stanford's Ted Shipkey recovered the ball. Stanford had the ball inside the Alabama red zone. With less than ten minutes on the clock, any type of score here by the Indians and the game would be over. On first down, Coach "Pop" Warner called a run off the left side by Hoffman for a three-yard gain. Another sweep around the left for one yard set up a third and six from Bama's thirteen yard line. On the next play, Stanford sent their 185-pound fullback Hoffman right up the gut for five yards.

It's a yard short from Alabama's seven yard line, and the clock was moving under seven minutes. A field goal would make it a two-score deficit for Alabama to overcome, but "Pop" wanted a touchdown.

Just prior to the fourth-down play, Wallace Wade quickly replaced the 165-pound Archie Taylor with the 200-pound Molton Smith to help clog the middle. Stanford snaps to Hoffman, who handed it to George Bogue on a reverse, but Bama was ready!

He didn't make it! It was Alabama's ball. But even after Alabama's goal-line stand, they could not move the ball. It seemed to be over.

The Tide continued to play hard, though, and the team was not about to give up. The clock showed three minutes to go, and Stanford was punting from the mid-field line. Wade called for a big rush on the punter. The ball was snapped back. Alabama's "Babe" Pearce broke through the middle and launched himself at the punter.

It's blocked!

The ball took a big bounce all the way back to the Stanford goal line, with all twenty-two on the field in hot pursuit. The punter Frank Wilton made a great play when he picked it up on the bounce at Stanford's goal line and moved the ball out to the fourteen before he was tackled.

Wade sent Holmes back in at center and moved Pearce back over to guard. Jimmie Johnson, who hadn't played all day due to a shoulder injury, was drafted into action. The clock was moving; it was Alabama's time to do or die.

Alabama shifted to the right side, leaving little doubt where the ball was going and who was going to carry it. Johnson carried the ball through the Stanford line for eleven yards, first and goal!

On the next play, Barnes takes the handoff to the left for a yard. On second and goal, Johnson moves to the right behind the crimson wave of Pickhard and Pearce and walks it into the end zone.

Touchdown Alabama!

Caldwell converted and the score with two minutes left was Stanford 7, Alabama 7.

But it wasn't over yet!

On the next series, Bama was able to hold Stanford to three and out, but the clock was about to hit zero. Stanford punted. Alabama surprised everyone when instead of going for the block they set up a return. Johnny Mack's little brother, Tolbert "Red" Brown, took the ball at his thirty and found his wall of blockers as the clock horn blew loudly. There was no time left, but the ball was still in play! Brown moved inside at mid-field to miss a couple of Stanford players, and he headed toward the end zone. He had passed everyone but the Fullerton, California, native Ted Shipkey. Shipkey remained calm and centered himself to hit Brown low. "Red" was nailed on the twenty yard line.

There were no tiebreakers in 1927. Game over: Stanford 7, Alabama 7.

### Postgame

If not Alabama, then who? That was the initial question, and I think we have at least narrowed it down to a few schools. Certainly as far as records go Stanford and Alabama were the leaders, having tied for the best records in the country before the bowl game. The two teams playing in the postseason Rose Bowl certainly earned a share of the title.

There is no doubt that Alabama was one of the elite college football programs from 1922 to 1926, with forty victories, which places them only two behind first-place Notre Dame during that span. Alabama led the nation in scoring during this five-year span and finished in the top three in defense every year, including the 1926 record of least points allowed (20). Alabama had the best overall record and the most wins of any school (big or small) in the nation from 1924 to 1926 and this included a twenty-game winning streak and the 1926 Rose Bowl victory. Coach Wade's record of twenty-six games without a loss was Alabama's school record for forty-six years.

This is clear evidence to suggest that Alabama earned at least a share of the 1927 championship. Let me end with a quote from Fred Digby, sports editor of the *New Orleans Item:* "The Alabama team brought new glory to the South and Southern football when it came from behind to tie the Stanford Cardinals at Pasadena on Saturday. Almost every expert in the east and west thought Stanford was too good for the Crimson Tide . . . But these experts worked along the line of thought that eastern and western football is superior to the southern brand. The result of the two Rose Bowl games, in which Alabama has figured: the victory over Washington in 1925 and the tie with Stanford proves a point we have been trying to make for years, football as played in the south is of as high caliber as football played anywhere."

He finishes with: "The entire south should be proud of the Alabama team, for it exemplifies the spirit of the southland."

The tradition was in place.

## NOTE

1. I used several different materials as my source, including period newspaper articles, books, and ESPN's *Encyclopedias of College Football,* but my major source was the *Spalding's* magazine. Their football guide was dividing schools into big or small classification before the NCAA. There were other undefeated schools. The exact number is impossible to know because complete records from all schools playing football in 1926 are not available. My best estimation is that there were about one hundred "small" schools, including Centenary College in Shreveport, Louisiana; New York University; and Lafayette College in Easton, Pennsylvania. These schools were not considered as "big schools," and even during perfect seasons they were not considered for postseason games.

# TABLE 2

## 1926

Coach Wallace Wade

National Champions, Southern Conference Champions

Won 9, Lost 0, Tied 1

| Alabama | Opponent | | Location | Date |
|---|---|---|---|---|
| 54 | Millsaps | 0 | Tuscaloosa | Sept. 24 |
| 19 | Vanderbilt | 7 | Nashville | Oct. 2 |
| 26 | Miss. State | 7 | Meridian, Miss. | Oct. 9 |
| 21 | Georgia Tech | 0 | Atlanta | Oct. 16 |
| 2 | Sewanee | 0 | Birmingham | Oct. 23 |
| 24 | LSU | 0 | Tuscaloosa | Oct. 30 |
| 14 | Kentucky | 0 | Birmingham | Nov. 6 |
| 49 | Florida | 0 | Montgomery | Nov. 13 |
| 33 | Georgia | 6 | Birmingham | Nov. 25 |
| 7 | Stanford | 7 | Rose Bowl | Jan. 1, 1927 |
| 249 | | 27 | | |

## CHAPTER THREE

# 1930

## Delbert Reed

Alabama's championship season of 1930 began with all the ingredients of a Hollywood movie script—a team fighting for glory after three lackluster seasons and a maligned coach on his way out but determined to salvage a sagging reputation—and it played out in black-and-white fairytale fashion, culminating in a crushing 24–0 Rose Bowl victory over Washington State that gave the Crimson Tide its third national championship in seven seasons.

Wallace Wade, the stoic head coach who had carried Alabama to two national titles and three Southern Conference crowns in seven seasons, stunned Tide fans in April by announcing that he would leave Alabama at the end of the 1930 season to become head coach and athletic director at Duke.

Wade said little about his reasons for leaving Alabama, but in resigning he recommended Georgia assistant and former Notre Dame quarterback Frank Thomas as his successor, and university president Dr. George Denny hired Thomas in July 1930. In their meeting, Dr. Denny provided Thomas with a hint of what lay in store for him at Alabama by saying, "It is my conviction that material is 90 percent, coaching ability 10 percent . . . you will be provided with the 90 percent and that you will be held to strict accounting for delivering the remaining 10 percent."[1]

Dr. Denny's words, called by Thomas the "coldest and hardest"

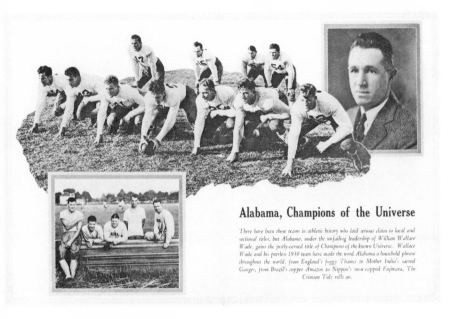

**Alabama, Champions of the Universe**

There have been those teams in athletic history who laid serious claim to local and
sectional titles, but Alabama, under the unfailing leadership of William Wallace
Wade, gains the justly-earned title of Champions of the known Universe. Wallace
Wade and his peerless 1930 team have made the word Alabama a household phrase
throughout the world, from England's foggy Thames to Mother India's sacred
Ganges, from Brazil's copper Amazon to Nippon's snow-capped Fujiwara, The
Crimson Tide rolls on.

The 1930 team was labeled by the campus yearbook "Champions of the
Universe."

he had ever heard, were a hint of what Thomas could expect as the
Alabama head coach.[2] The words might also help explain Wade's
departure following 5–4–1, 6–3, and 6–3 seasons despite his overall record of 51–13–3 and numerous championships after only
seven years at Alabama.

   Wade's impending departure cast a shadow over the 1930 season,
which forecasters predicted would be another mediocre one for the
Tide, but critics and forecasters were in for a lesson in Wade's determination and genius in one of Alabama's most-storied championship seasons.[3] The thirty-eight-year-old Wade produced what he
considered his best team ever as the Tide played to record crowds
at almost every stop during his farewell tour with the Crimson
Tide.[4]

   Wade set the stage for the Tide's inspired play in 1930 when he met with the team during preseason drills. "He called a team meeting . . . and it was an emotional one," John Henry "Flash" Suther, a senior halfback on the team, recalled nearly fifty years later.[5] "His remarks built a fire under us. Coach Wade said it would be his last year at Alabama because some of the radicals in the state didn't care for the way he was running things, then he gave us all a challenge, 'Gentlemen,' Coach Wade said, 'I'm gonna win this damn championship this season and if you want to be a part of it, you can. If not, get out of here now.' Well, we got with it. I mean we really buckled down and worked for him. . . . By the end of the year those radicals were begging Coach Wade to stay and it's obvious what he told them," Suther added.[6]

Alabama's defense, always a Wade trademark with 104 shutouts in 184 games at Alabama and Duke, was at its best in 1930. Anchored by All-America tackle Fred Sington, the defense allowed only 13 points in ten games for a record that stands today. In eight seasons at Alabama, four of Wade's teams allowed fewer than 30 points per season.

The 1930 team stood out for another reason, and that was Wade's famed "shock troops," a rugged second-team lineup that started eight of the Tide's ten games and played the first quarter while Wade and the first team sized up the situation. The plan worked to perfection, surprising most opponents and allowing the fresh, fired-up first team to rush in for quick scores in the second period.

By season's end, a team that started out with Sington as its only proven star, had placed nine players on various teams of honor, with Sington claiming a spot on every All-America list and Suther making several lists. John Cain, the sophomore signal caller and punting star who joined ten seniors on the first team, guard John Miller, and tackle Charles Clement joined Sington and Suther on the All-Southern team while quarterback John Campbell, guard Frank Howard, and ends Jimmy Moore and Albert Elmore earned honorable mentions.

Alabama offered a preview of things to come as it routed Howard College 43–0 in its opening game of the season at Denny Stadium. Suther, hobbled by injuries for two seasons, set the offensive
pace for the Tide as he led a fifteen-minute, 34-point scoring bar-
rage in the second period by rushing for ninety-one yards on four
plays and returning a kickoff ninety-six yards for a touchdown. His
rushing total, earned in only ten minutes of play, included a fifty-
five-yard scoring jaunt.

Wade's shock troops unit started and played all but the second
quarter as the Tide served notice that it would do anything but
throw in the towel on the season because of Wade's impending
departure. Alabama rushed for 515 yards, with Campbell getting
113, including a 53-yard scoring run. Hillman Holley, Cain, and
John Tucker also scored touchdowns on short runs, and Hugh
Barr Miller drop-kicked a thirty-three-yard field goal as part of
the scoring. The Tide defense allowed only three first downs in the
game.

The first known description of Alabama's bruising team of 1930
as "elephants" arose from the Tide's 64–0 pounding of Mississippi in Denny Stadium on October 4, and the label became more
popular as the season progressed. Wade used three full teams in
the easy win, but "had to throw heavy wraps over his Crimsons
Saturday to keep them from being charged with manslaughter,"
Birmingham's Zipp Newman wrote of the game.[7]

Alabama scored at will, with Joseph Causey (sixty-four yards),
Suther (fifty-eight), Campbell (forty-two), and Holley, Ralph McRight,
and Long (thirty yards each) rushing for touchdowns. Another
touchdown came on a twenty-five-yard pass from Moore to Ben
Smith.

Everett Stupper, a former Georgia Tech player who officiated the
Alabama-Ole Miss game and was greatly impressed with the size
and strength of the Tide, is credited with pinning the "elephant"

label on Alabama in a column written for the *Atlanta Journal* following the game.

"The Thin Red Line is a thing of the past, existing no more," he wrote. The Red Elephants have replaced it at the Capstone. Their every move reminds one of this mighty animal of the jungle. First their size, then their stampede charge reminded me of pictures that I had seen of this beast on wild charges in the jungle when he merely runs over by brute strength anything that might get in his way."[8] The "Red Elephants" tag caught on quickly among writers and broadcasters because of the size of the hefty Tide linemen and the elephant eventually became the team mascot.

Wade skipped the Crimson Tide's 25–0 victory over Sewanee in the third game of the season, choosing instead to personally scout Alabama's next opponent, the powerful and unbeaten Tennessee Volunteers, a team Wade had not beaten in two previous meetings.

Tide assistant Hank Crisp handled the team and followed Wade's script by playing the second team throughout the scoreless first quarter, then sending in the first team, which promptly scored on a fifty-eight-yard dash by Campbell to take a 6–0 halftime lead. Campbell added another touchdown; Tucker scored twice; and Miller drop-kicked a PAT to account for the final score.

Tennessee had lost only once since Bob Neyland became head coach of the Volunteers in 1926, and was unbeaten in thirty-four games (1927–1930) until the Crimson Tide stunned the Vols 18–6 before a record crowd of 20,000 in Alabama's homecoming game. Bleachers were brought in from area high schools to expand the 12,000-seat Denny Stadium as nine special trains brought fans from throughout the South to see the clash of southern football giants (Alabama vs. Tennessee and Wade vs. Neyland).

Wade's shock troops held Tennessee scoreless through the first period, then the speedy first team swarmed into the fray. Suther,

Campbell and Cain promptly led the Tide on a fifteen-play, eighty-one-yard drive capped by Cain's eighteen-yard scoring dash for a 6–0 lead. Suther added a thirty-one-yard touchdown on the next series to give Alabama a 12–0 halftime lead.

Reserve center Joe Sharpe recovered a Tennessee fumble at the Volunteers' thirteen yard line in the third period to set up Alabama's final score, which Campbell punched in from the one yard line. The Tide allowed its first score of the season late in the fourth quarter.

Suther carried only five times in the game but led all rushers with 100 yards, followed by 52 for Campbell and 39 by Cain. The Tide piled up 308 yards on the ground to 54 for the Vols, who added 151 through the air on the arm of quarterback Bobby Dodd.

Newman likened the Alabama line play against Tennessee to "a steam roller flattening out a freshly laid piece of paving. . . . It is doubtful whether Alabama has ever cut loose the unmerciful charge they leveled on Tennessee's guards and tackles," he wrote.[9]

Vanderbilt head coach Dan McGugin had personally scouted Alabama against Tennessee, and no doubt his report helped keep Alabama's offense in check as the Crimson Tide narrowly defeated the Commodores 12–7. But the Tide threw up an even stronger defense and continued its march toward a perfect season as 20,000 Legion Field fans watched.

Wade failed to start his rugged shock troops for the first time against Vanderbilt when McGugin let it be known that he would counter with his second team if Alabama's second unit opened the game.[10] Wade threw a different wrinkle into the game, however, by playing a six-man line and using an extra linebacker against the Commodores to all but shut down their running game as the Tide allowed only seventy-three yards rushing.

Campbell ran two yards for Alabama's first score in the second quarter and Suther dashed fifteen yards for another score in the third quarter following Newton Godfree's block of a Vanderbilt punt to give Alabama a 12–0 lead. Vanderbilt scored on a twenty-six-yard pass from Benny Parker to Bill Schwartz to make the final score 12–7. Cain's punting and outstanding linebacker play and the rushing of Suther (ninety yards rushing and a fifty-nine-yard kickoff return) and Campbell (ninety-five yards rushing) were keys to Alabama's win.

Nashville sportswriter Blinky Horn had high praise for Alabama following the game, writing that the Commodores were "pulverized by power, struck down by strength, swept aside by speed and crushed by cohesion. These Redmen are roguish people. They strike with venom."[11]

Horn seemed to raise his regard for Wade and the Alabama players a bit following the game as he wrote: "They have been talking for a long time about Alabama being not as nimble witted as some of their enemies, but today . . . the Bama Brigade was shrewd and cunning. If Bama is dumb, heaven help the Commodores when they encounter a smart team."[12]

A record crowd of 24,000 turned out in Lexington to witness another outstanding defensive effort by the Crimson Tide as Alabama shut out the previously unbeaten Wildcats 19–0 to push its record to 6–0 for the season. Suther rushed for 105 yards and caught a 49-yard touchdown pass from Jimmy Moore as the game's offensive star. Campbell and Long scored on one-yard plunges, and Whitworth kicked an extra point to account for the other scoring.

Alabama had 232 yards rushing and 85 yards passing on four completions in seven attempts while the Tide defense, led by Sington and Clement, held the Wildcats to 86 yards rushing and 48 passing.

The win was Wade's seventh straight over Kentucky, and one writer noted Wade's added incentive for defeating the Wildcats by recounting Wade's interview for the Kentucky head coaching job prior to joining Alabama in 1923: "It was winter time and bitter cold. Wade was left in a chilly corridor to await the committee's decision. It acted favorably on Wade, but in a discussion of other matters lost track of time, leaving Wade to shiver and freeze outside. Finally Wade decided that he had to act or freeze. He broke in on the meeting and dramatically informed the board that he had decided to withdraw as an applicant for the Kentucky coaching job. He said, 'Gentlemen, I have decided to go to Alabama, and I want to tell you that Alabama will beat Kentucky every year.' Then Wade stomped out of the room."[13] Wade kept his promise by going 7–0 against Kentucky at Alabama.

Alabama's defense was never better than in its 20–0 victory over Florida before 20,000 Gator homecoming fans in Gainesville. Wade used three teams, starting with his shock troops, and the Tide never allowed the Gators to advance beyond their own forty yard line.

Campbell scored on a 21-yard run for the Tide's first touchdown in the second quarter, then Campbell and Tucker added one-yard scores in the fourth quarter and Whitworth kicked two extra points to account for the scoring. Cain had 86 yards rushing, Suther 54, Campbell 59, and Tucker 39 as Alabama piled up 247 yards rushing and twelve first downs to only 47 yards rushing and one first down for the Gators.

Alabama's second- and third-stringers scored four touchdowns in the first half as the Crimson Tide coasted to an easy 33–0 victory over LSU for its eighth win of the season. Moore passed forty-five yards to Tucker for Alabama's first score, then Holley, Long, and Bellini scored touchdowns, and J. B. Whitworth kicked three extra points as Alabama rushed out to a 27–0 halftime lead. Campbell returned the second-half kickoff eighty-five yards for the final touchdown. Alabama's stingy defense held LSU to only two first downs in the game.

With a berth in the Rose Bowl and a chance for another national championship riding on the game, a sellout crowd of 28,000 packed Legion Field for the Crimson Tide's 13–0 victory over Georgia on Thanksgiving Day.

The game was a defensive brawl, but Campbell scored in the first quarter and added a TD and extra point in the final period to account for all the scoring as the Tide closed out a perfect 9–0 season to secure its third Rose Bowl invitation in six years.

Wade, set on avenging a 12–0 loss to the Bulldogs in 1929 and earning a shot at the championship he had vowed to win, didn't take any chances in a game with such high stakes. He started his first team and kept them in most of the game. Sington, playing every line position during the game, turned in one of his best games ever and recovered a Bulldog fumble in the process. Cain was at his best, also, rushing sixteen times for 120 yards and punting fourteen times for a 44-yard average. Suther gained 40 yards on ten tries, and Campbell added 42 yards on seventeen runs.

"Sington was a line in himself," Blinky Horn of the *Nashville Tennessean* wrote following the game. "It was his smashing work which broke down the Georgia air attack. . . . There have been great forwards in Dixie, but there has been no greater lineman than Freddie Sington," Horn added. He praised Cain's punting, saying Cain "dazzled, dazed and dizzied 28,000 fans with his fury on offense, defense and punting."[14]

Newman, in awarding the unofficial Southern Conference championship of 1930 to Alabama following the win over Georgia, wrote: "The Southern Conference is on record against naming a champion or giving trophies . . . yet public opinion has piled up an overwhelming decision in favor of the Red Elephants."[15] Alabama became the first team to play in three Rose Bowl games as it manhandled Washington State 24–0 on January 1, 1931, to claim its third national title.

Wade, who had played in the first Rose Bowl game for Brown in 1916, followed his usual script by starting his second team, much to the surprise of the Cougars and West Coast press. "It gave our regular backfield a chance to study Washington State's defense and I am sure that the reserves wore the Cougars down more than most people suspect," Wade said in explaining the use of his shock troops.[16]

The first team wasted no time in putting the game away, scoring 21 points in a seven-minute span as they hit the field running in the second quarter. The first score came on a sixty-four-yard pass from Moore to Suther, then Campbell added touchdowns of one and forty-two yards on Alabama's next two possessions and kicked all three extra points to account for 17 of the Tide's 24 points in earning most valuable player honors for the game. Alabama's final score came in the third quarter on a thirty-three-yard field goal by Whitworth.

Washington State's only serious scoring threat was thwarted on the Alabama four when Sington recovered a Cougar fumble. Alabama had 220 yards rushing and 92 passing (two of seven) to 143 rushing and 67 passing for the Cougars. Campbell gained 109 yards rushing while Holley added 48, Suther 34, and Long 26. Campbell's ball handling impressed the West Coast writers, causing one to write, "There was deception and sleight-of-hand hokus pokus going on that mystified the Cougars and delighted the spectators."[17]

"My boys came through splendidly," Wade said of the solid victory. "I'm glad to be able to leave Alabama with this as my last gesture in their behalf. Had we lost I guess certain folks would have felt a bit easier in mind about seeing me depart."[18]

Wade continued his winning ways at Duke, posting a 110–36–7 record. He carried unbeaten teams to the Rose Bowl twice but did not win another national title. Wade is remembered on the UA campus today with a street adjacent to Denny Stadium named Wallace Wade Avenue and his larger-than-life statue standing with Paul "Bear" Bryant, Frank Thomas, and Gene Stallings along the Walk of Champions near the University Boulevard entrance to Bryant-Denny Stadium.

## NOTES

1. Naylor Stone, *Coach Tommy of the Crimson Tide* (Birmingham, Ala.: Vulcan Press, Inc., 1954), 16.

2. Stone, *Coach Tommy of the Crimson Tide,* 16.

3. Paul Duncan, *Montgomery Advertiser,* Aug. 23, 1930.

4. Paul Lowery, *Los Angeles Times,* Jan. 1, 1931.

5. Al Browning, *Bowl Bama Bowl* (Huntsville, Ala.: Strode Publishers, Inc., 1977), 35.

6. Browning, *Bowl Bama Bowl,* 37.

7. Zipp Newman, *Birmingham News,* Oct. 5, 1930.

8. Everett Stupper, *Atlanta Journal,* Oct. 8, 1930.

9. Zipp Newman, *Birmingham News,* Oct. 19, 1930.

10. Zipp Newman, *Birmingham News,* Oct. 23, 1930.

11. Blinky Horn, *Nashville Tennessean,* Oct. 26, 1930.

12. Blinky Horn, *Nashville Tennessean,* Oct. 26, 1930.

13. Jimmy Burns, *Georgian,* Nov. 2, 1930.

14. Blinky Horn, *Nashville Tennessean,* Nov. 28, 1930.

15. Zipp Newman, *Birmingham News,* Nov. 28, 1930.

16. Zipp Newman, *Birmingham News,* Jan. 3, 1931.

17. Braven Dyer, *Los Angeles Times,* Jan. 2, 1931.

18. *Los Angeles Evening Herald,* Jan. 2, 1931.

## TABLE 3

### 1930

Coach Wallace Wade

National Champions, Southern Conference Champions

Won 10, Lost 0

| Alabama | Opponent | | Location | Date |
|---|---|---|---|---|
| 43 | Howard | 0 | Tuscaloosa | Sept. 27 |
| 64 | Mississippi | 0 | Tuscaloosa | Oct. 4 |
| 25 | Sewanee | 0 | Birmingham | Oct. 11 |
| 18 | Tennessee | 6 | Tuscaloosa | Oct. 18 |
| 12 | Vanderbilt | 7 | Birmingham | Oct. 25 |
| 19 | Kentucky | 0 | Lexington | Nov. 1 |
| 20 | Florida | 0 | Gainesville | Nov. 8 |
| 33 | LSU | 0 | Montgomery | Nov. 15 |
| 13 | Georgia | 0 | Birmingham | Nov. 27 |
| 24 | Washington State | 0 | Rose Bowl | Jan. 1, 1931 |
| 271 | | 13 | | |

## CHAPTER FOUR

# 1934

## MITCH DOBBS

**B**y the summer of 1934, faithful followers of Alabama football had already become accustomed to a steady red-meat diet of national championships, and hunger pangs were beginning to flair in Coach Frank Thomas's fourth year at Alabama. He was expected to feed the hungry. No one thought Thomas was a bad coach. No one called for his head or questioned his ability. But Thomas was a man who was under the gun from day one, if not before.

Thomas was hired in July 1930, a full thirteen months before he would ever coach a game. From 1927 to 1929, Alabama had three mediocre seasons under Wallace Wade. Depending on which source is consulted, Wade was either fed up with all the meddling and unforgiving expectations from UA president Dr. George Denny, or he was too thin-skinned to handle the constructive criticism, when he told Dr. Denny he would be leaving for Duke at the end of the 1930 season. In truth, it had to be a combination of both things that ushered in the Thomas era.

Before Thomas could start in '31 there was that little matter of the 1930 season to be dispensed with. When Wade turned his swan song into a 10–0 national championship season, with Thomas as an in-person observer laying low in the back of the train on the way to the Rose Bowl and having already been hired as Wade's hand-picked successor, Thomas inherited loftier expectations than

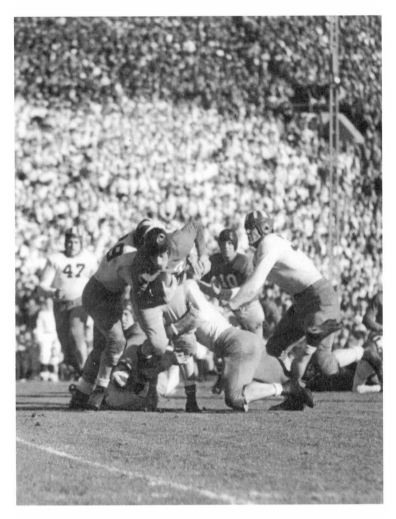

Stingy defense was the hallmark in 1934.

he could ever have imagined. It was in this context that Dr. Denny gave voice to his belief that football was 90 percent material and 10 percent coaching. Thomas would be provided the material and would be held strictly accountable for the remaining 10 percent, Denny said.

Needless to say, Thomas's claim that he would need some time to build a championship squad fell on deaf ears. By any reasonable standard, Thomas, who was thirty-three years old at the time of his first game as Alabama's coach, dealt with the pressure well. In his first three seasons, Thomas's teams won twenty-four games, lost just four, and tied one. Alabama was 9–1 in Thomas's first year, followed by an 8–2 record in '32 and a 7–1–1 mark in '33. But that just whetted the appetite—stoked the hunger. Would he ever get to the Rose Bowl riding in the front of the train?

As sportswriters sized up the 1934 team, there was great potential in the skill players: Joe Riley had most of the preseason buzz, though Millard "Dixie" Howell would end up with most of the glory. Both men were slightly built, but the reports were that Riley could really run the ball. Howell was slowed by injury, thus the early attention to Riley. Howell, a product of a small town in southeast Alabama called Hartford, was a passer, a ball carrier, and a great punter. His eighty-nine-yard punt against Tennessee in 1933 still stands as the longest in school history, but his greatest moments came in 1934.

Howell's main receiving target was end Don Hutson, a Pine Bluff, Arkansas, native who was the perfect combination of style and substance. Howell and Hutson were among the earliest to resemble a modern-day quarterback-receiver combo. James "Bubber" Nesbit, a newcomer from Bainbridge, Georgia, and Riley Smith from Columbia, Mississippi, a few miles north of Louisiana's eastern border, were generally used as blockers in the offensive backfield.

Bama had to replace veteran linemen, including All-America pick Tom Hupke. When Tennessee drove to the Tide six yard line, it was Hupke who stopped UT sensation Beattie Feathers for a pair of losses and then forced a bad pass on fourth down to secure Thomas's first victory over the Vols as well as the Tide's first SEC title.

But the "material" was there to do so effectively. In a note of great self-deprecation, an Atlanta writer recalled thinking that Alabama teams would eventually be lighter and more nimble in Thomas's Notre Dame Box than Wade's mammoth players who earned the "red elephants" nickname that has stuck around to the present day. Now they look more like rhinoceroses, he quipped, and the smaller ones might only be the size of mules—Thomas's '34 squad were every bit as imposing as its predecessors' under Wade.

Bill Lee, a lineman who would become an All-American that year, was selected team captain. Arthur "Tarzan" White, from Atmore, was a newcomer at offensive guard but capable. White made All-America in 1936. Paul "Bear" Bryant was called "the other end" by many writers, but that designation was not meant as a slight to Bryant. It was a tribute to Bryant's size and toughness in contrast to Hutson's skill and grace. Hutson and Bryant were widely considered to be the best pair of ends in southern football entering the 1934 season. They complemented one another perfectly.

Much like they are scheduled now, Alabama's season opener was a tune-up game. The first three games were a prelude to the annual make-or-break contest with Tennessee, which was always Alabama's biggest impediment to the national championship. Then if Alabama was fortunate enough to survive Neyland's bunch, the squad was expected to hang on each week for the rest of the regular season in hopes of a bowl trip.

The season started on September 29 with Birmingham's Howard College, which is now known as Samford, traveling to Tuscaloosa. The game was never really in doubt, and Alabama's first-quarter touchdown put the game virtually out of reach. Alabama scored a touchdown in each of the four quarters and failed to convert on all four of its extra-point opportunities. Senior back Joe Demyanovich scored two of the four touchdowns, while Riley and Howell had one apiece. The result was a 24–0 win in the opener.

The next weekend Alabama met Sewanee in Montgomery at the

Cramton Bowl, and the game went as expected, with the Tide winning 35–6. Dixie Howell dazzled Montgomery with touchdown runs of sixty-one and thirty-three yards. After the thirty-three-yarder that opened the scoring, James Dykes Angelich, from Indiana Harbor, Indiana, intercepted Sewanee's Ralph Ruch's pass and returned it twenty-three yards for another score. Ruch got Sewanee's only score on a spectacular play. Alabama was driving for its third touchdown, but Ruch intercepted a pass from Bama's Roy White at the thirteen yard line and picked up some well-timed blocks in returning it eighty-seven yards for a score. Alabama's lead was never threatened, however. Demyanovich plunged across the goal line to cap a drive spurred by first-year Dothan sophomore Young Boozer's running and passing in the third quarter, and Boozer found the end zone in the fourth quarter to cap the scoring.

The following week's game against Mississippi State in Tuscaloosa was even less of a contest and an embarrassment of riches for Bama's Young Boozer. He scored three touchdowns, including an eighty-yard kickoff return and a seventy-six-yard run from scrimmage. (In 1934, a team who had been scored upon had the option of receiving a kickoff or kicking off to the team that had just scored in an attempt to gain field position. It was not uncommon for a team that had been scored upon to elect to kick off.) Boozer capped another drive with an eight-yard run, and there were other big plays made by the Tide. Angelich scored on a forty-eight-yard run, and Riley Smith had a sixty-four-yard interception return for a score. Bryant's eleven-yard touchdown reception was the Tide's first passing touchdown of the year. A more perfect performance in anticipation of the biggest game of the year couldn't have been dreamed up.

But Tennessee was a different story altogether. The Vols' reputation was equal to Alabama's, and well deserved under Neyland. The previous year, the Tide went to Knoxville and took a 12–6 victory. In '34, the southern powers met in Birmingham and another slugfest was played. Alabama won with an impressive combination of defense and special teams play. The Tide took a 13–6 lead into the fourth quarter and held on for the victory when Kavanaugh "Kay" Francis, from Timson, Texas, dove into the line and stopped a Tennessee back short on a fourth-down run.

Demyanovich scored the game's first touchdown in the second quarter, and Hutson cut back and forth across the field on an end around for a nine-yard touchdown run. Bryant was ejected late in the first half after being penalized for "slugging," though a writer present said Bryant was nowhere near the incident. Shortly afterward, Tennessee's Charles "Pug" Vaughan passed the Vols to the two yard line to set up their only touchdown, a run by George Craig.

Dixie Howell was the star for Alabama, returning a punt for eighteen yards early, completing passes to Angelich and Hutson, including one for thirty-three yards that set up a touchdown, carrying the ball on offense, punting beautifully to flip field position in Alabama's favor, and making a touchdown-saving tackle in punt coverage in the fourth quarter. After the game Neyland called Howell the greatest back in the South.

Significantly, the forward pass was used with great success and helped establish Howell and Hutson as one of the great early passer-receiver combos. In 1968 Arnold Friberg created four paintings representing major turning points in the intercollegiate game. "The Passing Game: Alabama vs. Tennessee, 1934," depicted Howell and Hutson and was chosen to mark the beginning of a new era of offense.[1]

Alabama continued its season hosting Georgia in Birmingham the following week. Howell played only in the first half, carrying the ball fifteen times for 152 yards and two touchdowns. Angelich scored on a 38-yard run, and Demyanovich scored on a 2-yard run that was set up by Alex City's James Whatley's punt block. Georgia scored after a terrible punt gave Georgia field position at the Alabama 18.

Alabama traveled to Lexington, Kentucky, on November 3, and it proved to be the final time an Alabama opponent would score in the regular season. Alabama won 34–14. Howell-to-Hutson was in effect once again, as the pair connected on a twenty-two-yard pass to the Wildcat twenty yard line. Howell hit Angelich for fifteen more yards, and then ran to the two yard line, where Tilden "Happy" Campbell, from Pine Bluff, Arkansas, took the ball in. Riley scored on a sixteen-yard run in the second quarter, and Alabama took a two-touchdown lead into the half. Kentucky scored on a fifty-nine-yard drive in the second quarter and converted the extra point to cut into the lead. Bryant scored Alabama's third touchdown of the day on an end around in the fourth quarter, but Kentucky answered with a sixty-nine-yard run around left end by "Man O' War" Johnson. Riley hit Young Boozer for a thirty-eight-yard touchdown late in the game for the 34–14 final score. Hutson and Bryant got credit for solid games on offense and defense, as did their backups, ends Ralph Gandy and Jimmy Walker.

Eight thousand fans showed up at Denny Field for homecoming to watch Alabama's thrashing of Clemson, 40–0. Alabama scored a touchdown in each of the first three periods and tacked on three TDs in the fourth quarter. The Tide outgained Clemson 413–69, and had twenty-three first downs compared to just four for Clemson. Howell passed to Hutson for two touchdowns and rushed for another. Riley Smith scored on a quarterback sneak, and Young Boozer scored on an end around in the fourth quarter. Joe Riley scored on a thirty-yard run in the fourth quarter.

The crowd swelled to 14,000 the following week when Alabama traveled to Atlanta to take on Georgia Tech. The result was much the same, a 40–0 Tide victory highlighted by Dixie Howell's and Joe Riley's passing prowess. A Demyanovich touchdown was set up by a Howell-to-Hutson pass. Howell scored on a sixty-five-yard punt return in the second quarter and passed to Hutson for another touchdown minutes later. In the second half Riley Smith scored on a quarterback sneak, and a Bryant interception and a Howell-to-Hutson completion set up a five-yard end around touchdown run for Hutson. Demyanovich added an interception to aid the Tide shutout, and Clarence Rohrdanz made a touchdown-saving tackle on a sixty-eight-yard pass play by Georgia Tech.

The following week, 24,000 football fans gathered in Birmingham's Legion Field to see Howell's final regular season game, and Howell did not disappoint in leading Alabama to a 34–0 win over Vanderbilt. Howell punted for a 40-yard average, racked up 124 yards in punt returns, and ran for 162 yards and two touchdowns, receiving a rousing ovation as he left the game. Angelic scored on a touchdown run and on an interception return. Demyanovich added another rushing touchdown.

All sorts of pollsters weighed in at the end of the season, and Alabama was selected national champions by Billingsley, Boand, Dickinson, Litkenhous, Football Research, Helms, and the National Championship Foundation. Minnesota, who went 8–0 for the season, was also recognized as a national champion.

Though national champions had already been selected, Alabama's Rose Bowl bid to play Stanford was anything but unimportant. The Tide had its reputation to uphold. In three previous appearances against the West Coast power, Alabama was 2–0–1. The tie came on January 1, 1927, against Stanford. The January 1, 1935, Rose Bowl provided the opportunity for a rematch.

Thomas scheduled his squad's trip so they could arrive in Pasadena a full week early for the game. Many of the fans who couldn't afford the trip gathered at Tuscaloosa High School to get updates over a tickertape machine. There, the messages would be received and an Alabama cheerleader would signal whether the news was good or bad. The crowd reacted correspondingly. The news was mostly good. The crowd at the Rose Bowl was the largest in history, and the Howell-Hutson combination accounted for 24 of Alabama's 29 points.

The early part of the game was rife with Alabama turnovers. Angelich fumbled after an eight-yard run. After the defense held and got the ball back, Demyanovich fumbled, giving the ball right back to Stanford on Bama's twenty-five yard line. Bobby Grayson took advantage of the Tide mistakes, eventually scoring on a one-yard plunge. The extra point gave Stanford a 7–0 lead.

Howell led the Tide response. He returned a punt twenty-five yards, completed passes to Hutson for seventeen yards, Angelich for twelve, Bryant for sixteen, and then ran over the right tackle for a touchdown from the five. The extra point was no good, and the Tide trailed 7–6. Alabama took the ensuing kickoff to the twenty yard line where the drive stalled. Riley Smith attempted and made a field goal to give Alabama a 9–7 lead.

Then, after Howell returned the kickoff twenty-one yards to the twenty-six, and Angelich ran seven yards to the thirty-three, came the play that likely inspired legendary sportswriter Grantland Rice to write that Howell, "the human howitzer from Hartford, Ala., blasted the Rose Bowl dreams of Stanford today with one of the greatest all-around exhibitions football has ever known." Dixie Howell took the snap off right tackle, then cut back to the left, eluding Stanford defenders as he worked his way across and down the field. He picked up good blocking from his teammates and went in for the sixty-seven-yard score. The run gave Alabama a 16–7 lead. But Howell had to leave the game with stomach pains and was replaced by Joe Riley. Just before half, Riley Smith intercepted a Stanford pass, and with eight seconds left Joe Riley picked up the offense where Howell had left off. Riley passed deep for Hutson, who made an acrobatic catch at the fourteen yard line and went in for the score. Smith missed the extra point. At the half, Alabama led 22–7.

Grayson put Stanford back into contention in the third quarter leading a long drive to begin the second half. Elzo Van Dellen finished the drive with a twelve-yard touchdown run on a reverse, bringing the score to 22–13. Stanford forced a Bama punt, and Grayson was driving Stanford downfield when Kay Francis intercepted a pass thrown by Robert "Bones" Hamilton. Early in the fourth quarter, Howell put the final nail in Stanford's coffin with a sixty-nine-yard pass to Hutson for a touchdown. The pass traveled some forty yards by air, and Hutson ran the rest of the way from the thirty yard line, putting the Tide up 29–13. The teams traded turnovers later in the fourth quarter, and the game ended with no more scoring.

In the Tide's 1935 Rose Bowl win over Stanford, Howell completed nine of twelve passes for 160 yards, rushed for 11 more, and averaged 43.8 yards per six punts. Howell was a unanimous All-America selection, and later became a member of the all-time Rose Bowl team and the College Football Hall of Fame.

Hutson's performance in the 1935 Rose Bowl was indicative of his dominance. In that game, he caught six passes for 165 yards and scored on receptions of 59 and 54 yards in the 29–13 win over Stanford. Hutson was a unanimous All-America selection and later a charter member of the College and NFL Halls of Fame. He was selected to the all-time team for the first fifty years of Alabama football, and then in 1992, was elected to the Team of the Century. He was named NFL Player of the Year twice. Coach Thomas called him "the greatest player I've ever seen."

Alexander Ingram, a Tuscaloosa native and eighty-plus-year observer of Alabama football who saw all twelve of Alabama's national championship teams play, called Howell the best player in Alabama football history.

Tarzan White went on to obtain a doctorate degree from Columbia. He played in the NFL's very first Pro Bowl and was also a world champion professional wrestler.

Paul "Bear" Bryant was drafted professionally, but made his name as a preeminent college football coach. Bryant won six national championships and became college football's winningest Division I coach at his alma mater.

For Frank Thomas, the 1934 national championship was his first of two at Alabama. He compiled a 115–24–7 record. Thomas retired his position at Alabama after the 1946 season due to chronic health problems, though he continued to live in Tuscaloosa.

## NOTE

1. B & R Art Gallery (http://www.bnr-art.com).

# TABLE 4

## 1934

Coach Frank Thomas

National Champions, SEC Champions

Won 10, Lost 0

| Alabama | Opponent | | Location | Date |
|---|---|---|---|---|
| 24 | Howard | 0 | Tuscaloosa | Sept. 29 |
| 35 | Sewanee | 6 | Montgomery | Oct. 5 |
| 41 | Miss. State | 0 | Tuscaloosa | Oct. 13 |
| 13 | Tennessee | 6 | Birmingham | Oct. 20 |
| 26 | Georgia | 6 | Birmingham | Oct. 27 |
| 34 | Kentucky | 14 | Lexington | Nov. 3 |
| 40 | Clemson | 0 | Tuscaloosa | Nov. 10 |
| 40 | Georgia Tech | 0 | Atlanta | Nov. 17 |
| 34 | Vanderbilt | 0 | Birmingham | Nov. 29 |
| 29 | Stanford | 13 | Rose Bowl | Jan. 1, 1935 |
| 316 | | 45 | | |

# CHAPTER FIVE

# 1941

## WAYNE ATCHESON

The year 1941 was one of the most storied and spectacular in American sports history.

Joe Louis defended his heavyweight boxing title seven times. Joe DiMaggio hit safely in a record fifty-six consecutive games for the Yankees. Ted Williams hit .406 for the Red Sox, the last to top a .400 batting average. Whirlaway won the Triple Crown with Eddie Arcaro aboard. The Yankees and the Chicago Bears were major league and NFL champions. Lou Gehrig died at age thirty-seven of a disease later nicknamed for him.

The year ended with a shocking and unprecedented event in our nation's history. Japan attacked the United States at Pearl Harbor on December 7, changing the world for everyone. World War II had begun. American young men changed the course of history as the Greatest Generation went into war to win and did over the next three and a half years.

Weeks before the attack, Alabama would field a national championship football team. By now, the Crimson Tide had been to the Rose Bowl five times and had won four national championships. It had established itself as the South's football power. It had been only seven years since Bear Bryant and Don Hutson played in the national title game in 1934.

Coach Frank Thomas succeeded Wallace Wade as head coach ten years earlier. Thomas, a Muncie, Indiana, native, came with

A "Texas-style" celebration following the 1942 Cotton Bowl victory.

high credentials. As a Notre Dame quarterback for Knute Rockne, he was George "The Gipper" Gipp's roommate, a 1923 Law School graduate from the South Bend campus, and a real acquisition for Alabama from his backfield assistant job at Georgia. His philosophy was to "keep the players high and make practice a pleasure but not a lark. Be a disciplinarian, but not a slave-driver."

The Notre Dame box offense, with a shift to the left or right and the quarterback serving as a key blocker, was popularized down south. Coach Thomas was a wizard in coaching it. Imagine Alabama running a Notre Dame offense with an Irish coach!

Players played offense and defense, and many played the entire game. If a player came out, he couldn't go back in that quarter, except on timeouts, a new rule that year. Only a limited number lettered. Sophomores had to be really good to play. Facemasks would come a few years later. Black leather helmets with a single chin strap donned the courageous warriors' heads. Black high-top shoes were worn by linemen and backs. Baggy khaki colored pants with either white or crimson jerseys with small letters made up the uniforms. Pads were flimsy at best.

Coach Thomas's main concern in the summer was losing players to Uncle Sam. Hitler and the Nazis were stirring things up something fierce in countries like Lithuania, Poland, Holland, and the Netherlands. They were cruel toward Jewish people. Sure enough, six Alabama players were drafted or enlisted into the military service before the season began, including Don Hutson's younger twin brothers Ray and Robert, counted on for Tide duty in '41.

Tennessee had won three straight SEC titles, but the coaches and sports editors made Alabama the heavy favorite in 1941. In spite of losing twelve players to graduation, the draft, and academics, including starting quarterback Charley DeShane, who got married, Alabama was the conference favorite. Fall practice began with sixty players and thirteen returning lettermen. And it began without captain-elect John Hanson, a fullback from Roanoke, Alabama, who joined the service to become a war pilot.

It was the first time since 1932 that Alabama would play ten games, three each in Tuscaloosa and Birmingham, and six SEC games in a row. It was by far the most difficult schedule an Alabama team had faced in several years.

In ten years, Coach Thomas had posted an amazing 76–13–5

record with three SEC titles, had twice gone to the Rose Bowl, and had produced ten All-Americans. One of his assistants was Hank Crisp, beginning his twenty-second year on the Bama staff, while also serving as head basketball coach. The three other assistants were Red Drew, Tilden "Happy" Campbell, and Paul Burnum. Game-day coach attire was dark suits with vests, felt dress hats, and dress shoes, much the same apparel as bankers and attorneys.

The season didn't begin until September 27, but that gave Thomas and Drew the opportunity to scout Tennessee vs. Furman the week before in Knoxville. They scouted from the stands, legal in those days.

The Crimson Tide opened with Southwestern Louisiana coached by a great Alabama All-American John Cain (1930–1932), who had played for Thomas. The game kicked off on this "sultry summer afternoon," the Corolla said, at 3 P.M. Alabama won easily 47–6 on Denny Field with the starting lineup of nine returning lettermen and four starters.

The starting eleven were: LE Holt Rast (180, Birmingham); LT Mitchell Olenski (224, Vestal, NY); LG George Hecht (221, Chicago Heights, IL); C Joe Domnanovich (200, South Bend, IN); RG Tony Leon (195, Follansbee, WV); RT Noah Langdale (231, Valdosta, GA); RE James Roberts (185, Blytheville, AR); QB Al Sabo (185, Los Angeles, CA); LH Jimmy Nelson (183, Live Oak, FL); RH Dave Brown (188, Ensley); and FB Paul Spencer (197, Hampton, VA).

Amazingly, the Alabama starting eleven hailed from ten states. Alabama was the nation's number-one bowl team, playing in five Rose Bowls in the past sixteen years, and establishing itself as a football powerhouse. Thus, players were drawn to the Tuscaloosa campus to play for a winning program.

Touchdowns against Southwestern were scored by Paul Spencer (two), Jimmy Nelson, Don Salls, Dave Brown, Louie Scales, and guard Joe Chorba, a reserve guard, who "caught a blocked Bulldog punt and ambled 20 yards for a score." The Corolla also said,

"During the third and fourth periods, Coach Thomas gave his new candidates a chance to get game service and they completed the wrecking of the Bayou State team."

A stunning setback came the following week when Mississippi State pulled off the impossible. A touchdown favorite, Alabama had an afternoon filled with fumbles, pass interceptions, and blocked kicks and went down in defeat 14–0 in Denny Stadium before some 18,000 sweat-laden Tide fans. Bama's star-studded backfield got into scoring territory many times but stopped themselves with mistakes. They didn't have the spark needed, and bowl talk was suppressed. Of note, this series began in 1896 without missing a season of play.

Alabama took out its frustration against the Howard Bulldogs in Birmingham's Legion Field the following Saturday before 6,000 fans. In a 61–0 rout, Jimmy "Tater Head" Nelson returned the second-half kickoff ninety-five yards. Coach Thomas's third and fourth string scored 34 points in the fourth quarter. Howard kept its star halfback Jimmy Tarrant out of the game to prevent injury while the Tide was rolling.

Alabama's left halfback Ray Johnson from Birmingham was the smallest player in major college football at 5-2, 134 pounds. Late in the game, the sophomore completed five straight passes, the last for a twenty-two-yard touchdown to Ted Cook. Johnson then dropkicked the extra point. The popular young player was too small for ROTC but big enough for the football team.

Stadium capacity in Denny Stadium was 18,000 and Legion Field had 25,500 seats. On the sidelines, players and coaches sat orderly and erect on benches without backs. Coaches sometimes stood or kneeled. Both stadiums had a pole on the sideline with several loudspeakers for the public address system. Games were played with four officials.

In this era, Tennessee was Alabama's chief rival. The legendary Robert Neyland once said, "You never know what a football player is made of until he plays against Alabama." This game was huge. Alabama had lost to the Vols two straight years, and this battle was in Knoxville at Shields-Watkins Field. It would take a masterful effort, and that's what Alabama gave on this third Saturday in October before 37,000 fans.

Jimmy Nelson starred on offense, and Joe Domnanovich was the defensive star as Alabama squeezed out a 9–2 victory. Nelson intercepted three passes and his punting was brilliant, 44.6 yards per kick. Junior guard George Hecht booted a 23-yard field goal in the first quarter. Moments later, Holt Rast made a sensational catch of a Nelson pass for 22 yards that carried to the nine yard line where fullback Don Salls blasted off right tackle for the game's only TD. The extra point was blocked.

The Vols safety came late in the third quarter when Nelson fumbled a quick-kick attempt and was swarmed in the end zone. Alabama dominated the first half and held on in the second half as bowl talk reached new heights and Tennessee's bowl hopes dwindled. It was the Vols first home loss in four years.

The Alabama-Georgia game held just as much drama. It was Jimmy Nelson versus the great Frank Sinkwich, who was fourth for the Heisman Trophy in 1941 and who won the Heisman in 1942. Zipp Newman, sports editor of the *Birmingham News,* wrote that "trying to tackle Sinkwich is like trying to hold a wildcat."

The 23,000 fans who witnessed this 2 P.M. clash in Legion Field saw a classic. Alabama played brilliantly and won 27–14. Georgia was 3–0–1 and rated their best team since 1929. "Nelson and Sinkwich with their sensational sprinting and passing kept the crowd on edge all afternoon," Max Moseley of the *Montgomery Advertiser* wrote.

A fifty-nine-yard touchdown pass from Nelson to Holt Rast in the first quarter was followed by a sixty-seven-yard drive in five plays with Nelson scoring on a short run. Alabama jumped to a two-touchdown lead, and added another touchdown in the second quarter on a short thirty-one-yard drive with Paul Spencer scoring. It was 20–7 at halftime.

The second half saw Nelson knock down a Sinkwich pass on fourth down in the end zone. Moments later, Nelson intercepted a Sinkwich pass and returned it fifty-three yards for a touchdown. He even made Sinkwich miss trying to tackle him on his sensational return, as Coach Thomas clamped down on his cigar in the excitement.

Alabama was ahead 27–7 when Georgia, coached by Wally Butts, scored late against Bama's second and third stringers. Zipp Newman was inspired to write, "Surging like the Crimson Tide of 1934—the Rose Bowl champions of 1935—Alabama's Crimson stunned not only baffling [sic] Georgia . . . No Alabama team since the days of Dixie Howell to Don Hutson has played so well."

Even though outstarred by Nelson, Sinkwich with a broken jaw had fourteen more yards than the Alabama offense. But Alabama made no mistakes and capitalized on every break. Of Nelson, Coach Thomas said after the game, "I haven't seen one like him since Dixie Howell." Others praised for their play were Joe Domnanovich, Holt Rast, George Weeks, Mitchell Olenski, and Al Sabo.

Homecoming for Alabama's 4,921 students followed, and Alabama rolled over Kentucky that November 1 day 30–0 with reserves mostly on the field. It would be the last home game for seniors Jimmy Nelson, Holt Rast, Captain John Wyhonic, Noah Langdale, and Paul Spencer. The annual A-Club dance was a homecoming feature and the Million Dollar Band gave a 10 A.M. concert on the Union Building steps before the 2 P.M. kickoff.

Before the game started, President Richard Foster gave a brief address to the United States armed forces and dedicated the game to the armed services. All season, soldiers wearing their uniforms were admitted to the games for only fifty-five cents.

It was on to New Orleans where Alabama would face Tulane,

a powerhouse football team. It was billed to be the largest crowd (55,000) to ever witness a football game in the South. Some 15,000 soldiers from Camp Shelby, Mississippi, would attend.

A Thursday night pep rally of 5,000 students in Denny Stadium gave the team quite a sendoff. The team pulled away from the Tuscaloosa train station at 2 P.M. and arrived in New Orleans at 8:15 that evening. Alabama's band traveled by bus.

Tulane outplayed the Tide in the first half and led 14–6, even though in the first three minutes, Nelson took a punt and handed off to Dave Brown, who raced sixty-five yards for a touchdown. Not to be outdone, Alabama returned to the field five minutes before the third quarter started and their determination resulted in a seventy-five-yard drive with Nelson throwing to Rast for the final three yards to make it 14–13.

That score remained as both teams fought, clawed, and refused to give in. The play of the game was a sixty-six-yard quick-kick by Nelson midway in the fourth quarter to hold Tulane at bay. With four minutes remaining from Tulane's forty yard line, the play of Nelson, Rast, Russ Craft, and Don Salls punched the ball down to the seven yard line. With seconds remaining, Salls crashed into the end zone for a stunning 19–14 victory.

Zipp Newman wrote, "Tulane was probably the best SEC team Alabama ever beat. Alabama won on their great line play, strategy and courage." They played without Joe Domnanovich, who was injured, and Don Salls filled in for injured fullback Paul Spencer and played the entire game. A rising sophomore, Don Whitmire, was named SEC Sophomore of the Week. Alabama's bowl stock boomed.

Coach Bobby Dodd brought his Georgia Tech squad into Legion Field for another tough headliner on November 15. Alabama's record was 6–1. They made it seven wins with a 20–0 shutout before a crowd of 25,000.

Alabama led 7–0 at the half when Howard Hughes, understudy

to Nelson, scored from two yards out. Nelson started the third quarter in grand style with a sixty-eight-yard punt return, followed later when Hughes returned a punt seventy-one yards down to the four. Nelson passed to Russ Craft to complete the scoring.

Coach Burnum had scouted Tech three weeks earlier. He took his favorite bird dog "Jim." While staying overnight in Talladega, the dog broke from a building close to the hotel and Burnum had to leave without Jim.

It was a dismal next week for the Alabama faithful. University president Dr. Richard Foster, forty-six, died of creeping paralysis on Wednesday night, November 19. Alabama traveled to Nashville to face a fine Vanderbilt team at Dudley Field. They were met at the train station by Vandy assistant Paul "Bear" Bryant. In a driving rain and a field ankle deep in mud, Alabama lost 7–0. Rain came down in torrents, and the game was marred with ten fumbles.

Alabama reached the two yard line once and other scoring opportunities were stopped by a pesky Vandy defense. Alabama's defense was pushed to the wall many times but courageously allowed Coach Red Sanders's Vandy team only a thirteen-yard scoring pass in the third quarter. After six straight SEC games, Alabama regrouped and came back strong the next week at Miami.

It was Alabama's second night game in history. Nelson had a great game, returning a punt early for eighty-five yards setting up a Russ Craft TD run. Dave Brown burst for a twenty-nine-yard score in the second period, and Nelson had a short run completing a sixty-three-yard drive in the third stanza. Alabama rolled over the Hurricanes 21–7 for an 8–2 record. Don Salls played brilliantly the entire sixty minutes. By now, Nelson was being heralded as the South's best punter and passing threat and a great defensive back. As an all-star back, Nelson's jersey number was 73. Rast played like an All-American down the stretch.

On December 2, many were surprised when the Cotton Bowl officials extended an invitation for Alabama to face Texas A&M on

New Year's Day. But after a careful look at schedules of all competitors and with Alabama's bowl reputation, new president George Denny and Coach Thomas gladly accepted. Some considered A&M to be the best team in the nation.

Five days later on December 7, Japan shocked the world when it attacked Pearl Harbor. Third-term president Franklin Delano Roosevelt promptly delivered his famous "a date which will live in infamy" speech, and the United States had now entered World War II.

Duke coach Wallace Wade offered to host the Rose Bowl game in Durham, North Carolina. Oregon State agreed and beat undefeated Duke 20–16. In the other top-three bowl games, Georgia defeated TCU 40–26 in the Orange Bowl; Fordham downed Missouri 2–0 in the Sugar Bowl; and the best match-up was in the Cotton Bowl with Alabama and Texas A&M. Football expert Oswin K. King said, "If national ratings mean anything, you can bet that the Texas A&M and Alabama game overshadows any other bowl game."

Forty-nine Alabama players boarded the train for Dallas. The average team age was twenty-one, the average linemen weight was 195 and backs 176. The Million Dollar Band carried 90 students. Due to the war, only 1,500 Alabama fans made the trip. Once in Dallas, Alabama used the SMU stadium for workouts.

Alabama games were not on radio, but Mutual Radio Broadcasting carried the game nationwide thanks to Gillette, who sponsored the game for $7,500. Game tickets were "$4.40 to the end lines and $2.50 in end zones." The programs were 25 cents for this 1:15 kickoff.

Alabama was ready to put on a spectacular show to the 38,000 who huddled in blankets and gunnysacks on this subfreezing New Year's Day.

When day was done, Jimmy Nelson and company shocked A&M 29–21, and it wasn't that close. Alabama intercepted an incredible seven A&M passes and recovered five fumbles. The South-

west Conference champions were labeled the greatest passing out-
fit in the nation. A&M led in statistics, but the touchdowns were in
Alabama's favor. Bama built up a 29–7 lead when Coach Thomas
sent in his third- and fourth-string players. All forty-nine players
played.

Nelson ran a third-quarter punt back seventy-two yards "without a hand being put on him." Other scores came on short runs by
Nelson and Russ Craft, a pass interception by Rast, and a twenty-
two-yard field goal by Hecht. Alabama only had one first down the
entire day, but scores came in close range of the goal line due to
A&M mistakes. One headline read, "Tide Makes 29 Points on One
First Down." Nelson, Rast, and sophomore tackle Don Whitmire
were chosen MVPs for the game.

Alabama's check from Cotton Bowl officials was $44,502, which
was gladly received by business manager Jeff Coleman.

Alabama displayed the most convincing victory of all bowl winners by far. Despite a 9–2 record and while a majority of pollsters
chose Minnesota as national champions, *The Football Thesaurus,*
headed by Duke Houlgate, chose Alabama based on a system of
strength of schedule. Besides the solid victory over Southwest Conference champion Texas A&M, Alabama had significant wins over
Georgia (featuring Heisman winner Frank Sinkwich), Tennessee,
Tulane, Georgia Tech, and Miami. In ten regular season games, the
Crimson Tide gave up only nine touchdowns for 64 points.

Football ratings pollster Dr. E. E. Litkenhous said, "The Southeastern Conference is the strongest football organization in America
this year." Alabama proved to be the best in the league with wins
over the strongest SEC teams.

Holt Rast was chosen consensus All-American end, the same
honor center Joe Domnanovich would receive in 1942. Jimmy Nelson made second team All-American and first team All-SEC, as
did guard John Wyhonic and Rast. Guard George Hecht made
third-team All-SEC.

Don Whitmire of Decatur would become an All-American in

1942 and transfer to the Naval Academy where he would be an All-American, the nation's best lineman, and an admiral in the U.S. Navy. Senior tackle Noah Langdale had the distinction of graduating Phi Beta Kappa. Through the years, Nelson, Rast, and Whitmire have been selected for the all-time Cotton Bowl team.

Sports publicity director Rea Schuessler had good players and a great team to beat the drums for in '41. The team trainer was Bill Raney, and Joe Baker was the team manager.

This was a day when gasoline was 12 cents a gallon and a new car cost $850. A loaf of bread was 8 cents, and a gallon of milk cost 54 cents. It was the Big Band era and everyone loved Amos and Andy, the Grand Ole Opry, and Edward R. Murrow, all on radio, of course. Popular was Kate Smith's stirring song, "God Bless America."

The players of 1941 were a part of the Greatest Generation. Most went on to fight bravely in World War II. End Jimmy "Babs" Roberts paid the supreme sacrifice by giving his life for his country. Only a few players are living today, but all will forever be etched in Crimson fame. For sure, never forgotten, and "until in Heaven we meet."

# TABLE 5

**1941**

Coach Frank Thomas

National Champions

Won 9, Lost 2

| Alabama | Opponent | | Location | Date |
|---|---|---|---|---|
| 47 | SW Louisiana | 6 | Tuscaloosa | Sept. 27 |
| 0 | Miss. State | 14 | Tuscaloosa | Oct. 4 |
| 61 | Howard | 0 | Birmingham | Oct. 11 |
| 9 | Tennessee | 2 | Knoxville | Oct. 18 |
| 27 | Georgia | 14 | Birmingham | Oct. 25 |
| 30 | Kentucky | 0 | Tuscaloosa | Nov. 1 |
| 19 | Tulane | 14 | New Orleans | Nov. 8 |
| 20 | Georgia Tech | 0 | Birmingham | Nov. 15 |
| 0 | Vanderbilt | 7 | Nashville | Nov. 22 |
| 21 | Miami (Fla.) | 7 | Miami (N) | Nov. 28 |
| 29 | Texas A&M | 21 | Cotton Bowl | Jan. 1, 1942 |
| 263 | | 85 | | |

## CHAPTER SIX

# 1961
## The Resurrection

## WINSTON GROOM

The Crimson Tide roared onto the national college football scene in 1961 with the kind of flash and bang usually associated with electrical storms. It feared not, and it did not disappoint, and the fans rejoiced, for it had been a long time coming.

After the legendary teams of the great Frank Thomas in the 1930s and early 1940s, Bama's football fortunes at first had languished, then faltered, and then practically vanished. By 1957, the once-proud Rose Bowl contenders had won only four games during the previous three seasons and they had dropped from the national spotlight.

The players were undisciplined and disheartened, and an aura of failure loomed about them. They had lost faith in their coach, the hapless J. B. "Ears" Whitworth, and worse, the fans had lost faith in *them*. The games were sparsely attended; even the students began leaving before halftime.

For the faithful, the situation had become intolerable, and while it was clear that Whitworth must go, the question nagged—who on earth would replace him? What self-respecting coach of proven field merit would willingly place himself in the cellar—which was precisely where The University of Alabama football program was at the end of the 1957 season?

There was one distant prospect—a man who had been to the cel-

Coach Paul W. "Bear" Bryant enjoys a victory ride on his way to the national title in 1961.

lar, who knew what it was like, and who had climbed out through dint of toil and sweat and amazing force of character. This man owed much to the university, and it owned much to him, for he had left the canebreaks of Moro Bottom, Arkansas, in the 1930s to play end on Alabama's championship Rose Bowl team, and then gone on to coach at Maryland, Kentucky, and Texas A&M, where his first season had been a 1–9 disaster. Thus he was all too familiar with the cellar.

The man, of course, was Paul "Bear" Bryant, but when the star-studded Bama delegation finally approached him in 1957, it did so with trepidation, for when Whitworth's time had finally come,

Bryant's Texas Aggies had become the top-ranked team in the nation. But the Alabama committee need not have worried. Characteristically, when it came to the university, Bryant needed little persuasion. "Mama called," was how he expressed it at the time. He agreed to coach the Crimson Tide for ten years at an annual salary of $17,000 ($120,000 in today's dollars)—plus a house. There was no "buy-out clause." It turned out to be the best deal The University of Alabama ever made.

Even before he had coached his final game at A&M, Bryant flew to Tuscaloosa and addressed what would become his team of 1958. He told them straight out what to expect: previous seasons were behind them forever; total commitment was now required. They had to make their beds, make their grades, write their mamas, and say their prayers. He would provide them with everything else first class—but they had to *perform* first class or they were out. If they did those things, he promised, in four years they would win the national championship.

"I don't know any of you, and I don't want to know you," he told them. "I'll know who I want to know after spring training." Then he turned and walked out.

Thus, a new sun rose upon the most exhilarating chapter so far in the history of Alabama football. The fans had expected a Moses to lead the Crimson Tide out of the wilderness. What they got instead was God.

Some of the players were apprehensive because of Bryant's fierce reputation. Despite their dismal record on the football field, many of the players had enjoyed playing for Whitworth if for no other reason than because he treated them kindly and he ran a loose ship. However, dark rumors had preceded Bryant eastward, especially about how he had taken a hundred or so of his A&M players out to an abandoned army base hundreds of miles out in the desert and put them through the meat grinder. When he was finished, fewer than thirty team members remained. If that was what was in store at Alabama, it was generally agreed that hard times lay ahead.

Bryant put it more succinctly: "My plan was to bleed 'em and gut 'em because I didn't want any well-wishers hanging around. The team I inherited in 1958 was a fat, raggedy bunch. The best players, the ones with the most ability, quit us. But from that first day on you could tell this was a bunch of kids who were there with a purpose. I could just sense they were something special. I never had a group like that in my life."

And what a group they were! In '58 he brought them back to 5-4-1; in '59 to 7-2-2, a victory over Auburn, and a bowl game; in '60, to 8-1-2, another victory over Auburn, and another bowl game. Now he was poised to fulfill the pledge he had made three years earlier, when he promised them the national championship.

The ones who had been freshmen when Bryant had arrived were now seniors: Pat Trammell, Tommy Brooker, Red Wilkins, Ray Abruzzese, Curtis Crenshaw, Jimmy Sharpe, Richard Williamson, Jack Rutledge, Darwin Holt, Bill Battle, Billy Rice, Bill Oliver, Billy Richardson, and Billy Neighbors. (Bryant complained there were so many "Billys" on the team—there were nine of them—that every time he called out the name, half of the players would drop what they were doing and come running up to him.)

As well, a host of other, younger athletes would leave their mark that year: Lee Roy Jordan, Butch Wilson, Mal Moore, Mike Fracchia, Ed Vesprille, Cotton Clark, Jimmy Sharpe, Charley Pell, Butch Henry, Richard Williamson, Steve Wright, and Tim Davis—first of the great Davis brothers' place-kicking dynasty. (It is interesting to note, by way of comparison, that 80 percent of the '61 squad came from within the state, while barely half of today's players do.)

These men, by now presumably "bled and gutted," were thoroughly familiar with the "Bryant System" which, to some, had remained painfully mysterious—a fact that a mellower Bryant later admitted: "We lost some good boys when we first started at Alabama," he said in a *Sports Illustrated* interview a decade later. "If they'd known what I was thinking, what I had in mind—If I'd had the sense to *tell* them—they'd never have quit."

But that was then and these were the ones who took the field in the year of '61. By then Bryant had put up his famous coaching tower. It was a simple wooden affair, nothing like the Eiffel Tower-ish thing he would erect some years later. From there, he could survey his team and what he saw must have pleased him, even if it drew scorn and disdain from others in the football community.

"Just to look at them, you wouldn't think they belonged on the same field," said a scout from Georgia Tech, referring to the small size of the Alabama players. A coach at LSU actually thought Alabama was lying about the size of its team in the game-day programs, in order to throw opponents off their guard. If Bryant was bothered by such remarks he never said so; in fact, he seemed to relish them. His ideal squad was a picture of quickness, and his notion of fulfilling it was to recruit lean, mean, fast, high school fullbacks and tailbacks and turn them into guards and linebackers.

This worked splendidly for nearly a decade until the rules against holding were relaxed and schools—especially in the Midwest—began loading up their lines with men weighing 250 pounds or more. Bryant used to refer to them derisively as "big ole corn-fed boys" from Nebraska, but he got a wake-up call when Nebraska crushed the Tide in the 1971 Orange Bowl. After that he went off to find some big old corn-fed boys of his own, who would soon be dancing around out there with everybody else like Sumo wrestlers.

But that was well into the future, and the Crimson Tide of 1961 were quick as wildcats and twice as mean. The average weight of the line was barely 200 pounds per man, "dripping wet," and less for the backfield but they invariably beat opponents to the draw. (By contrast, Alabama's entire 1961 first-team offense weighed in collectively at 1,598 pounds—versus 2,412 for the 2007 offensive team. Put another way, fewer than 25 percent of the 1961 squad weighed more than 200 pounds. Today, 80 percent of the players exceed that weight.) Watching films of that season, it's amazing even today to see just how fast they were, coming off the line as if they were spring-loaded, and standing up their opposites like cardboard dummies to let their runners streak through.

There was another reason that Bryant was comfortable with having his players trim and rawboned. At the time, colleges were playing under the old NCAA rules of a modified two-platoon system, in which substitutions were limited; thus many of them would have to play both offense and defense, which might tire out men carrying a lot of beef.

In any case, when the Alabama team took the field in 1961 there was something electrifying in the air and everybody felt it, including this writer. It was my freshman year at the university and I was caught up in the excitement like everyone else: the pep rallies, the news coverage, the constant talk that this year we were going "all the way." The preseason polls had ranked the Tide high in the standings, and you could almost feel the confidence of the players when you saw them around campus: strong, sleek, agile, cunning, and most of all audacious, and ready to fall upon their opponents like a pack of hungry beasts.

Their first victims were the Bulldogs of Georgia, and even though it was nearly October, some claimed it was the hottest day on record in Athens. Nothing stirred, not even the faintest breeze, and in the stands fans prostrated by the settling heat, alcohol, or a combination of both, were carted off on stretchers like so many battle casualties. Nobody thought to take the temperature that had pancaked down upon the field, but it must have been an oven. Bama, however, wasn't fazed, and some suggested they might even have *liked* it hot, compared with what Bryant subjected them to on a regular basis during fall practices.

Led by the inimitable Pat Trammell at quarterback, the Tide struck first with a forty-one-yard Tim Davis field goal. It was the first time Alabama had recruited a player solely for his kicking ability; because of the limited substitution rules, place-kicking had always been relegated as a kind of "sideline" for players at other positions. The outstanding end Tommy Brooker, for instance, had been assigned the chore in prior years. But Bryant's decision to emphasize the importance of the kicking game had been a prescient one, for Davis earned his keep by racking up 49 points that year, and a total of 119 during his illustrious career.

Next, Trammell took the Tide down to the one, where the fabulous fullback from Memphis, Mike Fracchia, made one of his spectacular airborne plunges almost over the heads of the startled Bulldog defenders. Trammell then hit Butch Wilson for another touchdown, and Mal Moore threw to rangy Red Wilkins for another. The Bulldogs seemed stunned and helpless against the onslaught. In the second half Fracchia scored again with another aerial leap and Tim Davis connected with a field goal to end it, Bama 36, Bulldogs 6. It was a good start—a very satisfying start.

On the final day of September it was Tulane's turn. The game was traditionally played at night either in Mobile or New Orleans, and in the opening minutes in the Port City, Tommy Brooker took a Pat Trammell pass in for a score. It was also here that Bama employed the "quick-kick" to bamboozle the Green Wave. It was among the bag of tricks Bryant had brought with him to Alabama, and he used it with exceptional effectiveness. The quick-kick was a stratagem that harkened back to Bryant's own playing days in the 1930s when the "foot" in football meant more than it does now. Bryant realized early on that the team's offensive capability was less than dazzling, but that his defense knew no peers. Thus on third, second, and even *first* downs he would occasionally shock the opposing team by calling for a surprise punt—usually by halfback

Billy Richardson—that set the opposition on its heels far back in their own territory, where his powerful defense could—and often did—cause a fumble or interception.

In fact, in this game a Tulane player inadvertently touched the ball and Bama recovered. But after that, the game bogged down and the Tide seemed sluggish, until a Tim Davis field goal finally put them up 9–0 when the game ended.

Next week the men in crimson were back in their groove, rolling over Vanderbilt 35–6. Trammell put on a stellar performance, throwing, running, and calling tricky plays, including one that sprung Mike Fracchia for a sixty-eight-yard dash into the end zone. The interesting thing was that Trammell wasn't a flashy quarterback; his speed, running, and passing ability were about average. But what Pat had was heart and an extraordinary sense of what it took to win. And more than that, he knew what it took to get the other players to win, and Bryant himself called Trammell the greatest leader he ever coached. Beyond that, he was one of the most outstanding team leaders ever to play football at the university, right up there with Pooley Hubert and Harry Gilmer.

North Carolina State came up next with its legendary quarterback and future NFL star Roman Gabriel leading the Wolfpack. It was no match-up. Gabriel threw a touchdown pass but Trammell threw two and ran for a third and Davis kicked two field goals. Bama 26, NC State 7. The Tide got a scare when star fullback Mike Fracchia had his leg bent beneath him and was helped from the field while playing defense on a Bama goal-line stand. When everybody groaned while watching the replay next day, Bryant grumbled, "Hell, if he'd been charging forward like he was supposed to it wouldn't have happened."

Next week was a big one—Bama vs. Tennessee. The Tide hadn't won against them since 1954 and hadn't beat them at home since 1947. Now it was payback time. Home for big games in those days was Legion Field and the game was televised, which was a big deal then, before the advent of cable, since being on TV meant one of the three national networks.

On the by-now notorious "Third Saturday in October," the Tennessee Vols gave Alabama fans a fright in the first quarter with an amazing fifty-four-yard field goal, but that was all she wrote. Mike Fracchia blasted into the end zone for Bama's first score, and soon afterward Butch Wilson took a Trammell pass over the line for another. In the second period the irrepressible Tim Davis added 6 more points with his toe to end the half.

As for the rest of the game, Bama owned it, with Billy Richardson and Pat Trammell each scoring a TD. The remarkable Mssrs. Jordan, Neighbors, Pell, Holt, and others truly too numerous to mention held the hapless Vols to a mere sixty-one yards total offense. It was a victory sweet to savor, and Bryant began his long-standing tradition of passing out cigars to the winning players in the locker room, while the wretched Tennesseans slunk back to their buses for the long ride home.

Later it was revealed that during the pregame meal Bryant had entered the hotel dining room, locked the doors, had the tables removed, and ordered the defensive linebackers to practice "boosting" little Billy Richardson up into the air "as a human projectile" in hopes of blocking goals by Tennessee's renowned place-kicker. Bryant it seemed—and with good reason, considering Tennessee's fifty-four-yarder—had a last moment premonition that this was an area that might cause the team trouble. For his part, Richardson complained later that being thrown all over the dining room was worse than the licks he took on the field that afternoon.

By midseason Bama was ranked number four in the nation and the University of Houston wasn't supposed to be much competition, but it was. Pat Trammell threw for a touchdown and ran for another and Tim Davis's ever-reliable foot made it 17–0, but the Cougars scrapped and scrambled enough that the final score didn't accurately sum up the game. The Texans pushed right down to the Tide's goal line before an interception by Bill Battle set them back, and if Bama's number-one ranked defense hadn't been on its toes the result might have been different.

A rain-drenched homecoming crowd saw Alabama give the always-tough Mississippi State a 24–0 drubbing. The field was so slippery that the Tide could only throw for 70 yards, but more than made up for it with a 215-yard rushing spree. The next Saturday— which happened to be Armistice Day—Bama reveled in a carnival of scoring against underdog University of Richmond that might as well have served as a bye week. The Tidesmen posted more than 600 yards of total offense and Bryant played everybody on the bench in a 66–0 rout.

Here it may be interesting to note the way college football has evolved in the intervening years. During its 1961 championship season, the Crimson Tide gained nearly twice as many yards rushing as it did passing, but with today's teams, that ratio is almost completely reversed.

As the regular season wound down, Bama had only two more hurdles in order to become undefeated. The first was Georgia Tech and the second was Auburn. Tech was a tough customer in those days; even when they weren't in contention for the SEC title, they were a known spoiler. The Yellow Jackets showed up at Legion Field with fire in their eyes and the game quickly turned into a titanic defensive struggle that Alabama won by limiting the Engineers to a mere thirty yards rushing. In fact, they never got within the Tide's thirty-four yard line.

The game became notable, however, for an unfortunate incident on a punt in which Bama's star linebacker Darwin Holt hit Tech halfback Chick Graning with an elbow that fractured his jaw, broke his nose, and knocked out five of his teeth. The referee was standing within five feet of both players and watched the whole thing, but threw no flag. Nevertheless, the Atlanta press screamed bloody murder and Tech coach Bobby Dodd raised hell over the episode, which inspired the *Saturday Evening Post* to publish a nasty article by the *Atlanta Constitution* sportswriter Furman Bisher claiming that Bear Bryant taught dirty football. Bryant sued for libel, but the real storm broke a few months later when the *Post* followed up its original hatchet job with a story based on a report by a crackpot who claimed his phone line got mixed up with that of Bryant's and Georgia athletic director Wally Butts, in which he claimed he overheard the two coaches conspiring to fix the Bama-Georgia game (which Bama had won 35–0!), so they could bet on it.

This time, both Bryant and Butts sued for libel, and after the court awarded Butts $460,000 ($3 million today) the *Post's* parent company settled with Bryant for $300,000. It was said that the *Post* never recovered from the financial setback and it folded a few years later, but Bryant never quite got over this shabby treatment by the national media.

The season finale was of course Auburn and Bryant must have been as apprehensive as anyone against the hard-charging Tigers. He had lost his first two games to them, before squeaking by the previous year 3 to 0. But the Crimson Tide was now 9–0 and poised to become the national champion—provided they were not upset by the determined Plainsmen. As had been customary since the series was renewed in 1948, the showdown was at Legion Field— this time before the largest crowd ever to watch a football game in Alabama—and the Tide didn't disappoint. To start things off Darwin Holt recovered a Tiger fumble just minutes into the game to set up a Bama score.

After that, Pat Trammell marched the team up and down the field almost at will, with halfbacks Cotton Clark and Billy Richardson doing yeoman's work. Bryant's vaunted defense led by linemen Billy Neighbors, Charley Pell, and Tommy Brooker frustrated every Auburn attempt to score. Bill Oliver and Lee Roy Jordan were standouts in the defensive backfield, which intercepted four Auburn passes. Of Jordan, Bryant would say serenely: "If they stay between the sidelines, Lee Roy will get them." At the end it was Alabama 34, Auburn 0, and the Sugar Bowl—and with it the national title—lay in the balance.

On New Year's Day, 1962, The University of Alabama met nationally ranked Arkansas in the Sugar Bowl. The Razorbacks' offense was centered around future San Diego Chargers receiver and pro Hall-of-Famer Lance Alworth, and the betting was heavy that the Hogs would soon take to the air. Instead, they never even got off the ground.

On its first possession the Tide's Mike Fracchia ran a forty-three-yard dash to the Arkansas twelve where, next play, Pat Trammell rambled in for a touchdown. Just before the half Tim Davis added three points with a thirty-three-yard field goal. Alworth did manage to grab a twenty-two-yard catch in the third period to set up a Razorback field goal but that was the end of it—Bama 10, Hogs 3, and the undisputed national championship went to the Crimson Tide. Mike Fracchia was named most valuable player.

Alabama was awarded the MacArthur Bowl that year in recognition of the national honors. The trophy was presented by the aging general himself at a black-tie banquet in New York to Coach Bryant and Pat Trammell representing the team, and to Dr. Frank Rose and other school dignitaries representing the university. President John F. Kennedy was in attendance at the festivities and gave a heartfelt tribute to the Crimson Tide. Other honors were piled on: the SEC Championship, of course, went to Bama, and Bryant was named Coach of the Year by the National Association of Sportswriters. Lee Roy Jordan, Pat Trammell, and Billy Neighbors were made All-Americans, while Jordan, Neighbors, Tommy Brooker, and Mike Fracchia won All-SEC honors—a fitting climax to a perfect season. It didn't get any better than that.

The Crimson Tide of 1961 began like a well-oiled machine, afflicted at times by fits and starts, but by the end of the season it ticked with the precision of the finest Swiss watch. For their part, the players on that championship team distinguished themselves as well off the field as they had on it. Three of them, Jordan, Brooker, and Neighbors, went on to the pros, and later became successful businessmen. Tim Davis and Pat Trammell graduated from medical school, and Butch Wilson became a dentist. Red Wilkins became a lawyer, while others went into coaching, including Bill Battle, who made a notable career at West Point. Still others made their marks in investments or the manufacturing and building industries.

A sad event occurred not long before the tenth anniversary of the championship season. Dr. Pat Trammell, then a physician in Birmingham, was diagnosed with cancer and died the week after the team presented him with the game ball from a win over Auburn. He was always one of Bryant's favorites and Bryant wept bitterly, saying, "This is the saddest day of my life." Shortly before that, Trammell had told him, "Coach, don't feel sorry for me. I've had a wonderful 29 years."

Football had given Bryant his chance in life, and he made the most of it and gave back in full measure. He would have another quarter century at the university, covered in glory and national championships in a stadium that now bears his name, but he always said that those boys of '61 occupied the most special place in his heart.

# TABLE 6

## 1961

Coach Paul W. "Bear" Bryant

National Champions, SEC Champions

Won 11, Lost 0

| Alabama | Opponent | | Location | Date |
|---|---|---|---|---|
| 32 | Georgia | 6 | Athens | Sept. 23 |
| 9 | Tulane | 0 | Mobile (N) | Sept. 30 |
| 35 | Vanderbilt | 6 | Nashville (N) | Oct. 7 |
| 26 | N.C. State | 7 | Tuscaloosa | Oct. 14 |
| 34 | Tennessee | 3 | Birmingham (TV) | Oct. 21 |
| 17 | Houston | 0 | Houston (N) | Oct. 28 |
| 24 | Miss. State | 0 | Tuscaloosa | Nov. 4 |
| 66 | Richmond | 0 | Tuscaloosa | Nov. 11 |
| 10 | Georgia Tech | 0 | Birmingham | Nov. 18 |
| 34 | Auburn | 0 | Birmingham | Dec. 2 |
| 10 | Arkansas | 3 | Sugar Bowl | Jan. 1, 1962 |
| 297 | | 25 | | |

## CHAPTER SEVEN

# 1964

## TOM ROBERTS

**N**ineteen sixty-four . . . what a year! Lyndon Johnson was our president. George Wallace was the governor. And Paul "Bear" Bryant was the coach.

The Beatles were on Ed Sullivan; *Hello Dolly* and *Funny Girl* premiered on Broadway; and we went to the Bama Theatre to see *The Pink Panther.*

Americans were driving Ford Mustangs, flying in 727s for the first time, and eating new items to start the day: Lucky Charms, Pop-Tarts and Carnation Instant Breakfast. Other firsts during 1964 were the miniskirt, the topless bathing suit, the Birkenstock sandal, and the GI Joe action figure.

Here in the South, we had St. Louis Cardinals' baseball on KMOX from St. Louis and WTBC in Tuscaloosa; and we all celebrated when the Cards won the World Series. In Tuscaloosa, Joe Willie Namath and sixteen other Bama players were back for their senior year at Alabama. I, on the other hand, drove the forty-seven miles from Fayette to start my first year at the Capstone.

Wearing my only Madras shirt, I went through rush and pledged Sigma Chi, enrolled in the school of engineering, moved into a not-so-plush apartment on Tenth Avenue, and then made my way to Denny Stadium for the season opener on September 19 against the Georgia Bulldogs.

Coach Bryant's seventh team at Alabama went into the season

Ray Perkins and Joe Namath were two leaders of the 1964 champs.

ranked number four in the Associated Press poll. He would later
call this squad "my favorite team" in his first twenty years as a
head coach. As the media guide following the season pointed out,
"There wasn't exceptionally great talent on hand. There was great
dedication and oneness of purpose."

As fans, we saw that dedication as the Tide played one of the
toughest schedules ever, including eight Southeastern Conference
games. The first one came against Georgia under first-year head
coach Vince Dooley. He would produce champions during his tenure in Athens. On this late summer night, however, Dooley would
see just how good Namath could be. Namath threw for 222 yards
and ran for three touchdowns to earn national Back of the Week
honors.

Namath had plenty of help. Hudson Harris ran for a touchdown, and David Ray kicked a 27-yard field goal. And the Tide defense was stingy, giving up only 165 yards and a field goal to the Dogs. A sellout crowd of 43,000 saw Bama top Georgia, 31–3.

One week later, Bryant took the Tide to Mobile's Ladd Stadium to take on Tulane. The Green Wave held Namath in check for a quarter, but Joe Willie took over the rest of the way. He ran for two touchdowns and hit Ray with a thirty-three-yard touchdown pass. David added two field goals, and Frank Canterbury ran five yards for a touchdown. The Crimson Tide wiped out the Green Wave, 36–6.

October began with Bama's first game of the season at Legion Field in Birmingham. Forty-eight thousand fans braved the rain to see the Tide and Vanderbilt battle through a scoreless first half. In lousy weather, Bama's kicking team set up the first score: Paul Crane recovered a fumbled Commodores punt on the Vandy six. Namath quickly hit Harris with a two-yard touchdown pass and later ran fifteen yards himself for another score.

In the fourth quarter, Joe set a new school record for career touchdown passes, hooking up with Tommy Tolleson from nine yards out for a score. The Bama defense pitched its first shutout of the season, and the Tide went to 3–0 with a 24–0 win over Vanderbilt.

Back in Tuscaloosa, undefeated North Carolina State came calling. And we got a major scare when Namath went down with a knee injury early in the second quarter. It didn't happen in a violent collision or on a vicious tackle. Joe was running with the ball, made a sideline cut, and the knee just gave way. As Namath left the field, a defensive specialist named Steve Sloan came trotting in to take over at quarterback. Now Sloan definitely had experience at quarterback, and he had taken over for Namath before. When Coach Bryant suspended Joe for the 1964 Sugar Bowl, Steve had led Bama to a stunning upset of Ole Miss.

So it was no real surprise that the junior took over against the

Wolfpack and finished a scoring drive with a one-yard sneak to give Bama a 7–0 halftime lead. In the third quarter, Steve Bowman showed why he would lead the Tide in rushing; he scored from three yards out for a 14–0 advantage. Bowman, by the way, would finish the season with 536 yards on 106 carries. Sloan wrapped up the scoring for the Tide by tossing his first touchdown pass of the season, 10 yards to Tolleson. The defense came up strong, to say the least, holding the Wolfpack to just 84 yards, while posting its second shutout in a row and Bama knocked off North Carolina State, 21–0.

That brought us to my favorite day of any football season: the third Saturday in October and the annual battle with the Big Orange of Tennessee. Bama went to Knoxville looking for its fourth-straight win over the Vols, but the Tide traveled to the Smokies without Namath. That left the door open for Sloan, whose hometown of Cleveland, Tennessee, was just ninety minutes south of Neyland Stadium. He led Bama on two early scoring drives. One ended with a thirty-yard field goal by Ray. On the next drive, Sloan punched it in from a yard out to give Bama a 10–0 lead.

During his entire coaching career, Bryant put great emphasis on the kicking game, which always seemed to play a huge role in any Tide-Vol battle, and 1964 was certainly no different. Wayne Cook broke through to block a Tennessee punt, then Gaylon McCullough picked up the ball and ran twenty-two yards for a touchdown. Bama went to halftime on top, 16–0.

The Vols managed a touchdown in the second half, but eked out only 144 yards in total offense. Ray added a field goal in the fourth quarter, and the Crimson Tide had its fifth-straight win of the season, 19–8, over Tennessee.

Homecoming came to Tuscaloosa on October 24 with one of the best games in the history of the Southeastern Conference. Denny Stadium played host to a battle of unbeatens: 5–0 Alabama vs. 4–0 Florida.

Forty-five thousand fans saw the Gators recover a Bama fumble and get on the board first. Quarterback Steve Spurrier, just a sophomore, hit Randy Jackson for a touchdown and Florida led, 7–0. Bama's Sloan came right back, leading the Tide on an eighty-seven-yard scoring drive; Bowman capped it with a one-yard touchdown run. The Gators regained the lead in the third quarter, but Bowman answered one more time for Bama. From the Florida thirty, Steve blasted right up the middle and raced to the end zone to tie the game at 14–14.

The defense kept Spurrier and the Gators off the board in the fourth quarter, and the Tide won this epic battle when Ray kicked a twenty-one-yard field goal with 3:06 left in the game. Bama went to 6–0 with a 17–14 win over Florida.

I'm certain that Coach Bryant must have drilled one idea into his players the next week: you're ripe for an upset!

The third-ranked Tide headed to Jackson, Mississippi, to take on 3–3 Mississippi State. And you know the fans inside Memorial Stadium were roaring when the Bulldogs drove the length of the field on their opening drive for a touchdown. The Tide offense struggled, but did manage three field goals by Ray to go to halftime on top 9–6.

Bryant probably peeled some paint off the locker room walls because his players came roaring out in the third quarter to take charge. Bowman led the way, scoring two touchdowns in the third quarter as Bama rolled up 325 yards in total offense. By late afternoon, the Tide was headed home with its seventh-straight victory, 23–6 over Mississippi State.

November started with a top-ten showdown at Legion Field: undefeated and third-ranked Alabama taking on once-beaten and eighth-ranked LSU. A sellout crowd of 68,000 saw the Tide fumble a punt in the first quarter. The Tigers recovered at the Bama twenty-one and took just six plays to take a 6–0 lead on Doug Moreau's pass to Billy Ezell.

Sloan and the Tide roared right back to take the lead, Bowman going a yard for the touchdown. Ray added the extra point and Bama was on top 7–6. Moreau kicked a thirty-five-yard field goal to put the Tigers back in front, 9–7, and that's the way it stood until the fourth quarter. On the very first play, Ray kicked another field goal and Bama was ahead for good at 10–9.

Bryant left it up to his defense to salt this one away. Hudson Harris intercepted a Tiger pass and raced thirty-three yards to a touchdown for the final score of the night. There were other defensive heroes, however, in the final minutes: Frank McClendon knocked down three Tiger passes, and Ray ended LSU's hopes with another interception. Bama went to 8–0, and the win locked up the Tide's seventh SEC championship.

Coach Bryant took the Tide to Atlanta's Grant Field on November 14 to play archrival Georgia Tech in the final game of the series. And the coach had Namath back in the lineup, surprising Bama fans and shocking Yellow Jacket followers. Just before halftime, Mike Hopper recovered a Tech fumble at mid-field, and Joe came running onto the field. On third down, Namath hit David Ray, who took it all the way to the one. Bowman went in from there, Ray added the extra point, and Bama led 7–0.

Then came another surprise: an onside kick that Creed Gilmer gobbled up for the Tide at the Tech 48. Again, Namath went to the air, to Ogden to the three, and to Ray in the end zone. David's extra point sent Bama to halftime with a 14–0 lead.

In the third quarter, Ray kicked a field goal. Bama finished the scoring in the fourth when Bowman picked up a Hudson Harris fumble and jumped into the end zone. The Tide went to 9–0 with a 24–7 win over Georgia Tech, the 150th victory in Coach Bryant's career.

The season finale came on Thanksgiving Day and saw Bama come from behind to beat Auburn before 68,000 fans at Legion Field and millions more watching on television. The kicking game again was crucial. Auburn's center snapped the ball over his punter's head and Bowman raced down field to recover the ball in the end zone for a touchdown. Ray missed the extra point, then the Tide got off a short punt to give Auburn good field position at the Bama twenty-nine. Tucker Frederickson led the Tigers to the end zone, and they went to halftime on top 7–6. That set up Ogden for one of the great kickoff returns in Alabama history. He caught the ball in the end zone, headed to the hash marks and raced to the Auburn end of the field. Ogden hauled it 108 yards in all, but officially 100 for the touchdown. Sloan ran for a 2-point conversion, and Bama had the lead for good at 14–7.

An Auburn fumble set up the Tide's final score, with Namath hitting Ray Perkins on a twenty-three-yard touchdown pass. And Bama had finished a perfect regular season with a 21–14 victory over Auburn. And there was even more good news: Notre Dame lost to Southern Cal and Bama took over the number-one spot in the national polls. Both wire services, the Associated Press and the United Press International, named the Crimson Tide their national champions, the second of six titles under Coach Bryant. New Year's Day 1965 found Bama in Miami to face the Texas Longhorns in the Orange Bowl. The holiday found me in front of a TV set at Hank Hodo's home in Fayette to watch the first major bowl game ever played at night. And what a game we saw! Namath was the star of this one, though he didn't start the game because his knee was hurting so badly. The Longhorns raced out to a 14–0 lead before Joe took over at quarterback. He marched the Tide eighty-seven yards to a touchdown. Namath got it with a seven-yard pass to Wayne Trimble. The Longhorns came right back to go to halftime on top 21–7.

In the third quarter, Namath hooked up on quick passes to Tommy Tolleson, Wayne Cook, and Ray Perkins to move the Tide to the Longhorns' twenty. From there, he hit Perkins with a perfect strike for a touchdown. In the fourth quarter, another long drive for Namath and the Tide, but it bogged down and David Ray kicked a twenty-six-yard field goal to cut the Texas lead to 21–17.

Then the defense came up with the big turnover: Jimmy Fuller picked off a Longhorn pass and Bama was in business at the Texas thirty-four. Joe hit Ogden for seventeen and Bowman for six. Steve carried the ball for four, and the Tide had it at the two with three downs to get into the end zone. Bowman got a foot, then a yard, and then Namath went with the sneak on fourth down. Along with most Bama fans, I saw that Joe got in, but officials ruled he didn't. Tommy Nobis and the Longhorns stopped Namath, and Texas won the game, 21–17.

Media covering the game named Joe the Most Valuable Player in the game, an honor he richly deserved. The next morning, however, Joe became even more prominent. Sonny Werblin made him the highest paid pro player ever when he signed Namath to a $400,000 contract with the New York Jets.

Bama fans cheered for Joe in the pros, but he'll always be their idol for leading the 1964 team to the national championship. Namath and Ogden were the captains of a team that rolled up 250 points. On the defensive side, Bama allowed only 88 points with stellar play from the likes of All-American Dan Kearley, Mickey Andrews, Paul Crane, and Tim Bates.

And David Ray may have been the most versatile player on the '64 team. He led the team in three categories: receiving, interceptions, and scoring. The junior from Phenix City picked off three passes during the season. He caught passes from Sloan and Namath for 271 yards and two touchdowns. David finished second in the SEC in scoring with 71 points, but he set a new NCAA record for scoring by a kicker with 59 points on twenty-three PATs and twelve field goals. He was the AP's Specialist of the Year in the SEC.

Finally, let's not forget the terrific coaching staff that worked for Coach Bryant. Their names are legendary: Sam Bailey, Pat James, Dude Hennessey, Clem Gryska, Gene Stallings, Ken Meyer, Howard Schnellenberger, Jimmy Sharpe, Carney Laslie, and Hayden Riley. Three others were in their first year on the staff: Dee Powell, Richard Williamson, and Ken Donahue, perhaps Bama's all-time greatest defensive assistant. And since he did such great work in getting Namath back on the field, trainer Jim Goosetree deserves a mention; "Goose" was another Bama legend.

Their work and the play of the Crimson Tide certainly made my freshman year at Alabama a memorable one. And I must add a footnote: my older son, Elliott, enrolled as a freshman at Alabama twenty-eight years later. You know the rest of that story: Gene Stallings's 1992 Tide won Bama's twelfth national championship.

# TABLE 7

**1964**

Coach Paul W. "Bear" Bryant

National Champions, SEC Champions

Won 10, Lost 1

| Alabama | Opponent | | Location | Date |
|---|---|---|---|---|
| 31 | Georgia | 3 | Tuscaloosa (N) | Sept. 19 |
| 36 | Tulane | 6 | Mobile (N) | Sept. 26 |
| 24 | Vanderbilt | 0 | Birmingham (N) | Oct. 3 |
| 21 | N.C. State | 0 | Tuscaloosa | Oct. 10 |
| 19 | Tennessee | 8 | Knoxville | Oct. 17 |
| 17 | Florida | 14 | Tuscaloosa | Oct. 24 |
| 23 | Miss. State | 6 | Jackson (N) | Oct. 31 |
| 17 | LSU | 9 | Birmingham | Nov. 7 |
| 24 | Georgia Tech | 7 | Atlanta | Nov. 14 |
| 21 | Auburn | 14 | Birmingham (TV) | Nov. 26 |
| 17 | Texas | 21 | Orange Bowl (N) | Jan. 1, 1965 |
| 250 | | 88 | | |

## CHAPTER EIGHT

# 1965

## KEITH DUNNAVANT

**F**or a moment, Steve Sloan wondered if he was dreaming. It was the day before the 1966 Orange Bowl, the final game of his college football career, and as he stood on the deck of a cruise ship alongside his University of Alabama teammates, soaking up the final rays of 1965, the picturesque south Florida coastline drifted by in the distance. Several minutes into their ride around Miami Harbor, Alabama head coach Paul "Bear" Bryant pulled his quarterback aside and said, "Steve, I don't think we're going to be able to stop Nebraska. They have too much talent."

Sloan, a studious and soft-spoken senior from Cleveland, Tennessee, listened intently as Bryant spoke just above a whisper, so no one around them could overhear.

"I want you to throw any time you want to," Bryant told his quarterback. "You can throw from your one-yard line, their one-yard line . . . anywhere you want to . . . because we're going to have to score more points than we usually do to win this game."

Few messages could have shocked Sloan more at that moment than his coach telling him he could essentially pass at will, which repudiated everything he had been taught in Tuscaloosa.

Like all Alabama quarterbacks of the era, Sloan called the plays, but within a very rigid framework. Reflecting his philosophy that games were won with hard-nosed defenses and run-oriented of-

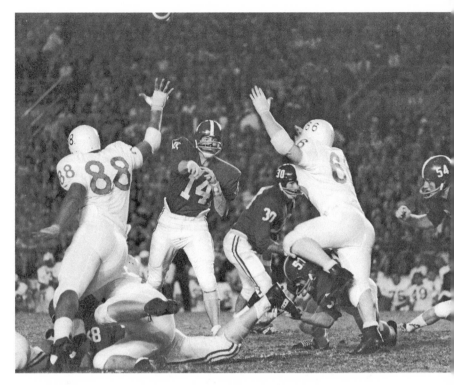

Steve Sloan led the Tide to an exciting culmination of the 1965 season, defeating Nebraska.

fenses that moved the chains efficiently without making careless mistakes, Bryant trained his quarterbacks to understand how to use the pass judiciously and sparingly. The Crimson Tide never passed on first down, and almost always ran the ball if it faced any less than second and six or third and six.

Now, with once-beaten, once-tied Alabama dreaming of a second straight national championship but facing a much larger Nebraska team favored by 17 points, Bryant was reaching outside his own comfort zone, displaying his pragmatism, in order to exploit Sloan's demonstrated passing skills.

"This was totally unheard of," Sloan said many years later. "I'd never heard him say anything like that before. Never. This was so foreign to how he had trained us to think. I was sort of speechless, hearing him tell me what he wanted me to do."

But, Sloan recalled, "If Coach Bryant believed that was the thing to do, I knew it had to be right. He just had a way of making you believe."

In 1965, more than anything else, the Crimson Tide believed.

After capturing the 1964 national championship—its second title in four years—Alabama was considered a legitimate contender once more. Ranked fifth in the preseason Associated Press poll, the Crimson Tide featured a seasoned cast on both sides of the ball, including All-America center Paul Crane, one of the best ever to play the position in Tuscaloosa; All-America quarterback Steve Sloan, who had seen significant playing time the previous year in relief of the injured Joe Namath; and several All-SEC selections, including fullback Steve Bowman, receiver Tommy Tolleson, defensive back Bobby Johns, and defensive lineman Creed Gilmer.

Like all Alabama teams of the era, the Crimson Tide was small but quick, especially along the offensive front, which was skinnier than many high school units. Still transitioning to the new two-platoon game, Bryant's team was stocked with players who had been recruited—and, subsequently, molded—to be able to go the distance without relief, which gave them all an iron-man quality that transcended the new rules. In an age before scholarship limitations, Bryant still signed sixty or more players in any given year, which loomed large across the entire program. Partially because Crimson Tide football maintained such a lofty status in the state's culture, he could push his players to their breaking points—and sometimes beyond—secure in that knowledge that every man who packed his bags, unwilling to take the punishment, inevitably would be replaced by a rugged soul who clung to his Alabama jersey as if his life depended on it.

Beyond strategy and tactics, Bryant taught his players how to fight, not just against some opponent who might be bigger, stronger, and more talented, but also against obstacles unseen, obstacles from within. The man who once played an entire game against Tennessee with a broken leg spent a significant amount of time training the minds of his players, teaching them to believe in him and in themselves, showing them how to think and act like over-achievers.

"So much of Coach Bryant's philosophy was built on the idea that if he made things tough on you, it would help you deal with adversity in all kinds of situations," said fullback Steve Bowman.

No championship team in Alabama history ever faced so much adversity as the 1965 Crimson Tide, and no championship team in Alabama history ever produced a more stunning object lesson about the power of faith and will in overcoming adversity.

In the nationally televised season opener at Georgia, number-five Alabama led the Bulldogs, 17–10, in the closing moments. It had been a tough, hard-fought game, contested on an unusually hot and humid night, but Alabama appeared in firm control. Then Georgia pulled off one of the most controversial plays in SEC history, as quarterback Kirby Moore passed to Pat Hodgson, who lateraled to Bob Taylor, who raced for a seventy-three-yard touchdown. The subsequent 2-point pass gave Georgia a stunning 18–17 victory.

Convinced that Hodgson's knees were on the ground when he batted the ball—meaning the play should have been called dead—Alabama fans howled in protest. The game film appeared to validate their position, but even when he saw it in black and white, Bryant refused to pout. He took the defeat like a man, but, believing the game never should have been so close, he proceeded to push his players relentlessly in practice over the next two weeks.

Tumbling out of the national rankings, the Crimson Tide rebounded by shutting out Tulane, 27–0, but Bryant kept testing his players' will. On the Monday before a pivotal showdown with powerful Ole Miss, he spent most of the day out of his famed tower, snatching, grabbing, challenging, sneering—motivating his young men to reach.

The next morning, he convened a practice before dawn and pushed even harder. "There wasn't anybody on that field who wasn't scared to death," recalled junior offensive lineman Byrd Williams.

Several players, unwilling to pay the price, quit the team, which was a central part of Bryant's grand plan. He wanted such players to pack their bags, before they contaminated the rest of the team. Those who remained were demonstrating their commitment to the cause, including junior offensive tackle Cecil Dowdy, who, like so many others, became a stronger and more determined football player when Bryant pushed him to the edge. During one drill, the coach rattled Dowdy's cage so forcefully, it left a scar that would linger, like a brand, for years.

In those tense moments, Bryant was leading his players back from the brink, though none of them quite understood it at the time.

"Coach Bryant challenged us, just when we needed it," Sloan said. "Somehow, he knew we needed to be challenged."

Trailing favored Ole Miss 9–0 at the half, the Crimson Tide rallied for a dramatic 17–16 victory. In the closing moments, the precise and methodical Sloan led Bama on a fourteen-play, eighty-eight-yard touchdown march, three times converting on fourth down, including a pivotal tackle-eligible pass to Jerry Duncan, a tenacious native of North Carolina who was destined to make the obscure gadget play famous.

"Beating Ole Miss the way we did gave us a lot of confidence at a time when we really needed it," Duncan said.

Two weeks later, after a 22–7 victory over Vanderbilt, Alabama was driving for the winning score in the closing moments against a good Tennessee team at Birmingham's Legion Field. Believing he was facing third down near the goal line, backup quarterback Kenny "Snake" Stabler mistakenly threw the ball out of bounds to stop the clock—on fourth down. The error—which would haunt Stabler for years—allowed Tennessee to escape with an unlikely 7–7 tie, and virtually every soul in the stadium believed Alabama's already flimsy national championship hopes had been mortally wounded.

Seething mad, Bryant arrived outside the Alabama locker room several minutes later to find the door padlocked. Imagine his frustration. His Crimson Tide has just bungled an opportunity to beat hated Tennessee, and he desperately needed to talk to his team in private, to seize control of a difficult situation before the season spiraled out of control. But the manager charged with unlocking the door had missed his most important assignment—yet another reflection on his usually fine-tuned organization—so for a few tense moments, the coach and his team stood impatiently in the shadow of the doorway.

Unable to convince his bodyguard to shoot off the lock, the fifty-two-year-old Bryant, whose massive frame towered over the entire team, told his players to move away from the door. Lowering his shoulder, he rammed the door once, then again, and to the astonishment of every player and coach standing nearby, the hinges collapsed. One by one, they started filing through the dislodged door.

"That's one of those things that, if you hadn't seen it with your own eyes, you might not believe it," recalled Jerry Duncan.

Fully expecting a tongue-lashing, the Alabama players quickly took their seats and listened intently as Bryant assumed complete responsibility for the tie. He told them it was all his fault, especially Stabler's throw at the end, which he said resulted from confusion on the sideline.

"But you can still win the national championship, if you think you can," he said. "Unless I've misjudged you."

Instead of coming away from the scene demoralized by how they had allowed their season to go awry, the Alabama players found Bryant's response inspiring. Especially in the context of what they had learned about themselves during those difficult days after the loss to Georgia, Bryant's little speech infused every man on the team with a renewed sense of possibility and responsibility. The message was clear: "I believe in you. The question is: How bad do you want it?"

The reality was much more complicated, because the odds of Alabama rebounding from a 3-1-1 start to claim a second straight national championship seemed astronomical. No team had ever won the big prize after suffering a loss and a tie.

Determined to battle back into the hunt, Alabama knocked off Florida State (21-0), Mississippi State (10-7), LSU (31-7), and South Carolina (35-14). Meanwhile, several early contenders suffered second losses, including Texas, Southern Cal, and Notre Dame. After crushing archrival Auburn (30-3)—which clinched the school's third SEC title in five years—the Crimson Tide climbed to fourth in both the Associated Press's poll of sportswriters and the United Press International's poll of coaches.

Since the beginning of the AP poll in 1936, the national champion had been named prior to the bowl games, a practice also shared by the UPI poll, which joined the mythical crowning game in 1950. Often, this antiquated, irrational approach to the bowl system had undermined faith in the process, including 1964, when Texas upset national champion Alabama in the Orange Bowl, 21-17. But 1965 represented a turning point in college football history. In what was billed as an experiment, the AP decided to hold its final vote after the bowl games for the first time, a decision that infused the 1965 postseason with a whole new level of meaning.

Sensing an opportunity, Bryant convened a meeting of his seniors and listened as they expressed a desire to accept an invitation to play in the Cotton Bowl, which was perfectly understandable, considering they had played in the Sugar and Orange Bowls the two previous years.

"Cotton Bowl?" he interrupted, shaking his head.

Moving over to his chalkboard, Bryant diagramed the most bizarre day in bowl history. He told his players UCLA would upset undefeated, number-one-ranked Michigan State in the Rose Bowl; LSU would go to the Cotton Bowl and shock undefeated, number-two-ranked Arkansas; and by accepting an invitation to the Orange Bowl, Alabama could capture the national title by knocking off undefeated, number-three-ranked Nebraska.

"Coach Bryant was very convincing, as he always was," said senior linebacker Jackie Sherrill. "I don't think we truly appreciated as a team how unprecedented that kind of scenario was. All that mattered to us was having the chance to win the national championship."

Two days before the Orange Bowl, being billed in the press as an enormous mismatch, Bryant caused a stir with his rugged but skinny offensive linemen by refusing to have his picture taken alongside them.

"I don't want to be seen with those scrawny little guys," he said, loud enough for all to hear. "They're going to get their asses whipped."

The comment landed with a mighty thud.

"I never will forget how much it hurt to hear him say that . . . how much I wanted to show him," recalled junior offensive guard Johnny Calvert.

Bingo. Mission accomplished.

With huge and talented Nebraska outweighing Alabama by more than thirty pounds per man, especially along the front line, the game looked like a certain rout. Bryant even took the time to apologize to his players—for scheduling them to play such a clearly superior team.

But the coach wasn't belittling his quick little boys. He was reaching inside their heads and motivating them, because he understood they needed all the mental ammunition he could muster to overcome the physical mismatch.

What followed was one of the biggest upsets in bowl history.

Catching Nebraska completely by surprise, Alabama dominated the Cornhuskers from the opening kickoff. It was 24–7 at the half.

Taking his coach's instructions to heart, Sloan—already named the SEC Player of the Year by the *Nashville Banner*—shattered most of the Orange Bowl's passing records, looking brilliant while completing twenty passes for 296 yards. The MVP trophy he took home easily could have been shared by the offensive line, which somehow manhandled the much larger Nebraska defensive front. Ray Perkins, a junior receiver from Petal, Mississippi, made his name known to a national television audience by recording an Orange Bowl record nine catches, including two for touchdowns. Lineman Jerry Duncan kept befuddling the Cornhuskers by catching one tackle-eligible pass after another. The Crimson Tide even used the onsides kick as a potent offensive weapon. With the game firmly in hand just before halftime, Sloan—who had already attempted twenty-five passes—trotted back to the huddle to find a replacement lineman sent in by the boss.

"Steve, Coach Bryant says you don't have to throw on *every down!*" the substitute said, unaware of their maritime summit.

Nebraska managed some offensive fireworks of its own in the second half, but Alabama's stunning 39–28 victory was never in doubt.

Bryant's bold decision to scrap his conservative philosophy for one game would rank as perhaps the greatest strategic triumph of his entire career.

"Alabama is outstanding," Nebraska head coach Bob Devaney said. "As far as I'm concerned, they have the best football team in the country."

Bryant, who said he was "overjoyed at the way this football team performed," noted that he didn't have a vote in the AP poll. "But I wish I did," he said with a smile.

As Bryant predicted, all three undefeated teams lost on New Year's Day, so two days later, when the Alabama players woke up to the news that they had been awarded the national championship by the Associated Press, the full measure of their unlikely journey began to sink in.

More than the greatest comeback in the history of the national championship process, 9–1–1 Alabama's 1965 trophy struck many members of the Crimson Tide as a validation of something deeper.

"We got knocked down, had some adversity, and only then did we truly find out what we were made of as a team," remarked Jerry Duncan. "We kept fighting and we kept believing, and I think the experience of going through that season taught all of us so much about competing in life."

# TABLE 8

## 1965

Coach Paul W. "Bear" Bryant

National Champions, SEC Champions

Won 9, Lost 1, Tied 1

| Alabama | Opponent | | Location | Date |
|---|---|---|---|---|
| 17 | Georgia | 18 | Athens (TV) | Sept. 18 |
| 27 | Tulane | 0 | Mobile (N) | Sept. 25 |
| 17 | Mississippi | 16 | Birmingham (N) | Oct. 2 |
| 22 | Vanderbilt | 7 | Nashville (N) | Oct. 9 |
| 7 | Tennessee | 7 | Birmingham | Oct. 16 |
| 21 | Florida State | 0 | Tuscaloosa | Oct. 23 |
| 10 | Miss. State | 7 | Jackson (N) | Oct. 30 |
| 31 | LSU | 7 | Baton Rouge (TV) | Nov. 6 |
| 35 | South Carolina | 14 | Tuscaloosa | Nov. 13 |
| 30 | Auburn | 3 | Birmingham | Nov. 27 |
| 39 | Nebraska | 28 | Orange Bowl (N) | Jan. 1, 1966 |
| 256 | | 107 | | |

## CHAPTER NINE

# 1973

## JOHN DAVID BRILEY

$\mathbf{P}$aul Bryant was entering his sixteenth season as the head coach of the Alabama Crimson Tide,
having won three national championships in the 1960s—1961,
1964, and 1965—and narrowly missing two others in 1962 and
1966. However, by the end of the decade the veteran head coach
had become complacent by going 6–5 and 6–5–1 in 1969 and 1970.
Bryant had become so frustrated with his own performance after
the 1969 season that he almost left college football for the professional ranks and the Miami Dolphins. After watching an offense that was rarely productive in the spring of 1971, Bryant visited his old friend Darrell Royal at the University of Texas and
learned about the new wishbone offense that Royal had imple-
mented three seasons earlier with great success. The Bear really
rolled the dice three and a half weeks before the opener of the 1971
season by secretly putting in the wishbone. The switch paid imme-
diate dividends as the Crimson Tide stunned the world in the Los
Angeles Coliseum by defeating third-ranked Southern California
17–10 and presented Bryant with his two hundredth win as a head
coach. Alabama went on to go 21–3 in the next two seasons, winning back-to-back Southeastern Conference championships, and
two top-five finishes in the final national polls. Going into the 1973
season, it was unclear which direction the Tide would take.

With thirteen starters and thirty-five returning letterman, most

Woodrow Lowe stalks a Georgia back.

serious observers of college football thought that Alabama would
be a strong contender for SEC and national honors. The Skywriters
(writers around the Southeastern Conference) picked Bama as a
solid second behind Tennessee for winning the conference championship, while the Associated Press picked the Crimson Tide sixth
in their preseason national poll. Bryant was not impressed with
any of this as he talked to the Skywriters eleven days before the
season opener with the University of California. He outlined the
problems to the writers by stating: "We look like a 5–5 right now
and I am not kidding . . . . If we can get everybody well and have
them out six or seven weeks, I think we can have a football team.
Starters or lettermen don't mean a thing. The important thing is
how many winning football players you have and we don't have
many right now."[1]

The sixth-ranked Crimson Tide were considered to be strong favorites over a Cal team that featured future offensive National Football League stars such as Vince Ferragamo, Steve Bartkowski, and Chuck Muncie. Needless to say, the only offensive stars on this September 15 opener were from The University of Alabama. Alabama rolled up 667 yards of total offense, setting a new school record and winning by the score of 66–0. It was a well-balanced attack for a wishbone offense that had 405 yards rushing and 262 yards passing. Gary Rutledge and Richard Todd split the quarterbacking duties, with both playing excellent games.

The defense limited the high-powered California offense to only 250 yards and no points. Woodrow Lowe led the stubborn Bama defense with eight tackles, four assists, and an interception. Lowe was awarded the AP's Southeastern Lineman of the Week with his stellar performance in his first start of his career. Coach Bryant was quite liberal in his praise for the Phenix City sophomore: "He was reckless and all over the field. He made every tackle early in the game. He was just everywhere." Later on, the veteran head coach called Lowe "the best linebacker I've had since Lee Roy Jordan."[2] Alabama would jump to fourth in the AP poll after the blowout over the University of California.

Paul Bryant returned to Lexington for the first time in nearly twenty years after he left the University of Kentucky at the conclusion of the 1953 season. The pesky Wildcats lay in wait for their biggest home game in a number of years. It would be the first game played in the new Commonwealth Stadium and all 54,100 seats were sold for Bryant's return.

Alabama struggled in the first half, trailing 14–0 at halftime. Whatever Paul Bryant said at halftime must have awakened his team. Willie Shelby took the opening kickoff one hundred yards for the Tide's first touchdown. The Crimson Tide offense scored 21 unanswered points in a 28–14 victory. The defense led by Mike DuBose, Woodrow Lowe, and Chuck Strickland was superb in the second half, allowing only one first down in the first conference win of the season.

Alabama dropped to fifth in the national rankings as they traveled to the "Music City" for the third game of the season against the Vanderbilt Commodores. Former Crimson Tide quarterback Steve Sloan may have been the coach for this spirited Vanderbilt squad, but Vandy was no match for the Red Elephants as the Tide rolled to a 44–0 sinking of the Commodores. Alabama used fifty-three players in the first quarter to jump out to a 17–0 lead and never looked back. Fourteen Tide running backs carried the ball for 416 yards and were led by Wilbur Jackson's 69 on only seven carries.

The Georgia Bulldogs came into Tuscaloosa thinking that they could take the third-ranked Crimson Tide. Alabama led 13–3 at halftime but should have scored at least two more times. This looked like one of those games that if they did not perk up soon in the second half, they would lose it. Alabama almost did as they fell behind Georgia 14–13 with three minutes to go in the game before Gary Rutledge and company went to work. He completed a couple of passes, and Willie Shelby exploded for a thirty-six-yard run before Rutledge scored on an eight-yard scamper with about two minutes to go to give the Tide the lead. Shelby's run on the 2-point conversion extended the Alabama advantage to 21–14. However, the men in Crimson were not through. They scored again on Randy Billingsley's seventeen-yard run. The Tide ultimately prevailed 28–14, but not without a big scare. The game ended as Wayne Rhodes deflected a Georgia pass for an incompletion. On the way down several frustrated Bulldog players fell on the Bama defensive back and starting punching him wildly. Conley Duncan saw what was going on and decided to seek some revenge for his fallen comrade. The Alabama linebacker stated that "I was just getting ready to haul off and hit a few of these guys when I saw out of the corner of my eye 10 or 12 Georgia players right on my heels. I knew right then that Coach Bryant's warning against fighting during the game was good advice."[3] This victory gave a good Alabama team a lot of confidence because they were down late in the contest, but were able to come back and ultimately win the game.

Alabama traveled to Gainesville to meet the Florida Gators for the fifth game of the season. The Crimson Tide won 35–14, but the game was much closer than the score indicated. Bama led in first downs 16–13, total yardage 248–223, which was over 200 yards under their average for the season, and the score was only 21–14 going into the fourth quarter. Alabama moved up to number two in the rankings after their victory over the Gators. Ohio State was ranked number one.

The "Third Saturday in October" would be played before a packed house of over 72,000 in Legion Field and a national television audience. Both Alabama and Tennessee were undefeated through five games. The tenth-ranked Volunteers came into Birmingham looking for an upset. Whoever won this game had a leg up in winning the conference championship and kept their hopes alive for a national title.

The game started off with a bang as Gary Rutledge hit Wayne Wheeler for an eighty-yard touchdown pass on the first play from scrimmage. Wilbur Jackson scored from the eight to make it 14–0 after the first quarter. Tennessee came roaring back with two touchdowns of their own in the second quarter. Willie Shelby caught an eleven-yard pass for the Tide's third score. The score at halftime was 21–14, Alabama.

Tennessee received the second-half kickoff and tied the game in only five plays. Condredge Holloway, the slippery quarterback from Huntsville, hit Mitchell Gravitt for a sixty-four-yard touchdown to tie the game at 21. The rest of the third quarter was a draw as both teams went into the final quarter deadlocked.

The first five minutes of the last quarter was a beauty for Alabama and a disaster for the Volunteers. Robin Cary took a Tennessee punt 64 yards for a touchdown to put the Tide up 28–21. The

Crimson Tide defense stiffened and held the Vols on the next possession. Wilbur Jackson took a pitch around right end and spun around to the other side of the field for an 80-yard touchdown run. Suddenly, Bama leads Tennessee 35–21. On the ensuing kickoff, Conley Duncan stripped Stanley Morgan of the ball and Alabama recovered. Three plays later, Paul Spivey went over from the three to make it 42–21. The Crimson Tide hung on the rest of the way to go to 6–0. This was the fourth time this season that the offense gained over 400 yards—524 to be exact. Wilbur Jackson had his personal best for the Tide by gaining 145 yards on twelve carries. He also was named AP's Southeastern Back of the Week for his stellar performance against the Volunteers.

The Hokies of Virginia Tech came into Tuscaloosa with a 1–6 record against the number-two-ranked Crimson Tide, fresh off of their biggest win of the year. Paul Bryant was not sitting on his laurels when he told the players that "we need to prepare for this game like it was the Rose Bowl."[4] They listened to Bryant and responded in kind with a 77–6 shellacking of Virginia Tech. Alabama gained 833 yards of total offense, of which 748 yards were on the ground. Four Tide runners went over the 100-yard mark: James Taylor 142, Wilbur Jackson 138, Calvin Culliver 127, and Richard Todd 106. Alabama set NCAA records for total yardage and rushing yards; the third and fourth teams played most of the second half. Bryant said after the game that he was proud of his players for winning the game but "was embarrassed by the score."[5]

Former Alabama assistant coach Bob Tyler was now the head coach for the Mississippi State Bulldogs, and he had had first-hand experience with the Tide offense. Tyler may have known the potential weaknesses of this offense, but it was not apparent in the 35–0 drubbing that his Bulldogs suffered in Jackson, Mississippi. The Crimson Tide used sixty-nine players and amassed 487 yards of total offense in their third shutout of the season. Alabama moved to 8–0 and remained second in both polls.

The Miami Hurricanes came into Tuscaloosa with a 5–3 record that included a win over the University of Texas and a loss to the Oklahoma Sooners in the final two minutes, 24–20. Both of these two opponents ran the wishbone offense very effectively and Oklahoma was ranked in the top five in the country. Alabama had to focus on the Hurricanes for their homecoming game and not look past that. Luckily for the Tide fans, they did not, and they won 43–13. The Alabama offense was somewhat inconsistent, but Gary Rutledge did throw two touchdown passes. They were aided on the special teams for a number of big plays in their ninth victory of the season, including a block punt for a safety and two punt returns for touchdowns, one for fifty-two yards by Willie Shelby, and another sixty-two-yarder by Duffy Boles.

Thanksgiving night in Baton Rouge, Louisiana, was the sight of two undefeated Southeastern Conference teams seeking the SEC championship and still in the hunt for the mythical national title. The game was televised nationally by ABC. The LSU Tigers came into the game 9–0 and ranked seventh in the country, while their counterparts had the same record with a second national ranking. In nine games, Alabama averaged over 44 points and 500 yards a game. They also led the league in scoring defense by allowing only 8.6 points a game. LSU was averaging 28.1 points and only giving up 13.9 points per game.

Alabama would get a sterling performance from Gary Rutledge that ultimately got him on the cover of *Sports Illustrated* the following week. The Birmingham junior ran 11 yards for a touchdown and passed for two others, one to George Pugh and the other to Wayne Wheeler in the 21–7 victory. Rutledge was four of five for 166 yards and ran for 60 yards on thirteen carries. He would later call this game "the best of my career."[6] The Crimson Tide led 14–0 at halftime and extended the lead to 21–0. Ricky Davis had two interceptions, and Woodrow Lowe led the Alabama defense that limited the LSU offense to a quarter of their average point production in the 21–7 victory. Ohio State tied Michigan on Saturday, and Alabama catapulted to the number-one ranking in both the AP and UPI polls. Rutledge and Lowe were named Southeastern Back and Lineman of the Week for their efforts against LSU.

Greg Gantt came into this game leading the nation in punting with a 49-yard average on twenty-four punts. The Birmingham senior was looking for revenge in this game from the two blocked kicks in the final five minutes of the game that resulted in a 17–16 Auburn victory. As it turned out, Gantt only had to punt once but got to kick off six times in the 35–0 Alabama drubbing of their in-state rival. Alabama rolled up over 400 yards of total offense with a number of offensive stars sharing in the honors. Wilbur Jackson led the Tide rushing attack with 89 yards on fifteen carries. Randy Billingsley chipped in with 66 yards on ten carries. Both running backs scored a touchdown in the Alabama rout. Gary Rutledge was again brilliant at quarterback, scoring two other touchdowns. The Crimson Tide defense turned in their fourth shutout of the season, never allowing Auburn past its thirty-four yard line. Wilbur Jackson earned Player of the Game honors from ABC, who televised the game nationally. On the following Tuesday the Crimson Tide kept the number-one ranking in both polls. UPI awarded Alabama the national championship, while AP would crown its champion to the winner of the Sugar Bowl between the Tide and the Fighting Irish of Notre Dame on New Year's Eve.

The Sugar Bowl game of 1973 will go down as one of the most exciting in the history of college football. It was the first meeting of the two most prominent college football programs ever. The game itself lived up to all of the pregame hype as the two teams each had three different leads during the game but could not hold these as the contest went down to the final minute. The first quarter was all Notre Dame, with two good offensive drives that resulted in two field goals and a 6–0 lead. Their defense held the explosive Alabama offense to no first downs in the opening period. The Crimson

Tide offense got rolling in the second half and drove sixty-three yards from its own twenty before fumbling away a scoring opportunity. They got the ball back after a Notre Dame fumble at its own forty-eight and drove down the field with Randy Billingsley scoring from the six yard line. Bill Davis's kick made it 7–6. Al Hunter took the Alabama kickoff and ran ninety-three yards to give the Fighting Irish a 14–7 lead. Davis kicked a thirty-nine-yard field goal to narrow the Notre Dame lead to 14–10 at halftime.

The game went back and forth in the second half just like it had in the first. Alabama took a 17–14 lead in the third quarter only to see Notre Dame surge ahead 21–17 going into the final period. The Crimson Tide scored on a twenty-five-yard halfback pass from Mike Stock to Richard Todd to take back the lead 23–21 as Davis missed the extra point. Bob Thomas kicked a nineteen-yard field goal with 4:26 to go in the game to give the Fighting Irish a 24–23 lead. Alabama got the ball back but could not garner any offense and had to punt the ball away. Greg Gantt boomed one sixty-nine yards that backed up Notre Dame to its own one yard line. The Tide defense stiffened and held the Irish to two yards on the next two plays, which set up a third-and-eight call from their own three yard line. Tom Clements calmly dropped back in the end zone and hit Robin Weber with a thirty-five-yard pass that gave Notre Dame a first down with less than two minutes to play. It was one of those four or five plays that Coach Bryant had talked about in the past that separate two evenly matched teams in a big game. Bryant would tell his defeated Crimson Tide team that he did not think that "they had lost the game but that time just ran out on us."[7] This game was truly one for the ages.

Although Alabama lost this 24–23 thriller and the Associated Press National Championship with it, they still accomplished a number of good things during this 11–1 season. They did win the UPI National Championship. The Crimson Tide won their third-straight SEC championship with a winning margin of 24.5 points, the most in conference history, and the offense set eleven school records during the season. The '73 squad had six first- or second-team All-Americans, and nine made the All-SEC first team. This was Paul Bryant's best offensive team in history and only one point separated it from his best team ever. In the history of Alabama football, 1973 was indeed one to remember.

## NOTES

1. Delbert Reed, "Stand Close to Panic Button," *Tuscaloosa News,* September 5, 1973, 17.

2. Tom Saladino, "Reckless Woodrow Earns SE Laurels," *Tuscaloosa News,* September 18, 1973, 9.

3. Conley Duncan, interview with the author, Tuscaloosa, Alabama, November 16, 2000.

4. Delbert Reed, "Rose Bowl Time Bryant Declares," *Tuscaloosa News,* October 23, 1973, 8.

5. Jimmy Bryan, "Bryant Embarrassed as His Machine Gets in Gear, Can't Stop," *Birmingham News,* October 28, 1973, 14C.

6. Gary Rutledge, interview with the author, Birmingham, Alabama, June 3, 2007.

7. The author was a student trainer for The University of Alabama during the 1973 football season. He was present in the locker room after the game when this quote was made by Paul W. Bryant.

# TABLE 9

## 1973

Coach Paul W. "Bear" Bryant

UPI National Champions, SEC Champions

Won 11, Lost 1

| Alabama | Opponent | | Location | Date |
|---|---|---|---|---|
| 66 | California | 0 | Birmingham (N) | Sept. 15 |
| 28 | Kentucky | 14 | Lexington | Sept. 22 |
| 44 | Vanderbilt | 0 | Nashville (N) | Sept. 29 |
| 28 | Georgia | 14 | Tuscaloosa | Oct. 6 |
| 35 | Florida | 14 | Gainesville | Oct. 13 |
| 42 | Tennessee | 21 | Birmingham (TV) | Oct. 20 |
| 77 | Virginia Tech | 6 | Tuscaloosa (N) | Oct. 27 |
| 35 | Miss. State | 0 | Jackson (N) | Nov. 3 |
| 43 | Miami | 13 | Tuscaloosa | Nov. 17 |
| 21 | LSU | 7 | Baton Rouge (N,TV) | Nov. 22 |
| 35 | Auburn | 0 | Birmingham (N) | Dec. 1 |
| 23 | Notre Dame | 24 | Sugar Bowl (N,TV) | Dec. 3 |
| 477 | | 113 | | |

## CHAPTER TEN

# 1978

## KIRK MCNAIR

**M**ore than any other Alabama national championship season, the title won by the 1978 Crimson Tide team is defined by one play. That play came in 1979, on January 1 in the Sugar Bowl. Even those who didn't see it know of "The Goal Line Stand." It lives in Alabama football lore, an exceptional and important series in the national championship game—number-one Penn State against number-two Alabama. And it was symbolic of that physical contest.

The series, however, did not come at the end of the game. It was midway through the fourth quarter and the Nittany Lions of Coach Joe Paterno would have other opportunities. Still, the defensive stand fit the 1978 Crimson Tide team like a houndstooth hat fit its famous coach.

There were three great plays in the defensive stop, setting up fourth and goal at about the one foot line. Penn State quarterback Chuck Fusina was looking over the situation. Fusina and Alabama defensive tackle Marty Lyons had become acquainted at an All-America event a few weeks earlier.

"He said, 'How close is it, Marty?'" Lyons said.

"I said, 'Chuck, it's about 10 inches. You'd better pass.'"

The drama of the advice was exceeded only by the crunch of reality. The Lions tried a run and the defense held.

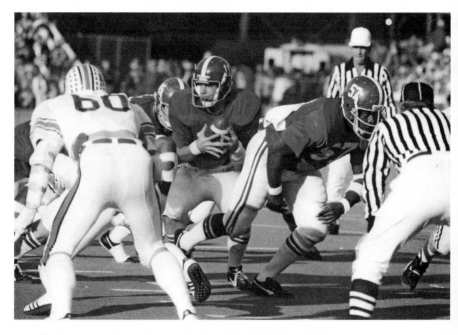

Dwight Stevenson clears the way for Bama's wishbone attack.


As it turned out, there was no more scoring. Alabama carried the day, 14–7, and won the consensus national championship.

Victory in the Sugar Bowl was the completion of the title trip. Where did it begin?

Esoterically, it began as far back as the 1920s, when the president, Dr. George Denny, decided football could be important to the university. Or maybe the journey to victory began in 1958 when Paul Bryant was hired as head football coach, or in 1971 when Bama changed its offense to the wishbone, or even in 1977, when Alabama seemed to have rebounded from a first-game loss. Many thought a 35–6 rout of Woody Hayes's Ohio State would earn Bama a championship, but the Tide was poll-vaulted by Notre Dame.

That 1977 team featured two of the great offensive players in

Alabama history, Hall of Fame receiver Ozzie Newsome and full-back Johnny Davis.

Alabama ordinarily played a lot of men in games during the Bryant wishbone era. In 1978 there was very little change from the lineup that started the season to the starters against Penn State in the Sugar Bowl. Keith Pugh had replaced Newsome at split end, and Steve Whitman took over for Davis at fullback. Mike Brock and Vince Boothe had moved up from backups in 1977 to starters in 1978 at the guard positions, and Buddy Aydelette was a new starter at tackle. Returning starters on offense were Rick Neal at tight end, Jim Bunch at right tackle, Jeff Rutledge at quarterback, and Tony Nathan at left halfback. Major Ogilvie had been one of a handful splitting time at right halfback in 1977, and as a sophomore in 1978 he was the starter.

It was an experienced defense. Wayne Hamilton was back at defensive end; Marty Lyons and David Hannah were the returning tackles; Barry Krauss and Rich Wingo were the veteran linebackers; and strong safety Murray Legg and left cornerback Don McNeal were returnees in the secondary. New men included Warren Lyles replacing Terry Jones at noseguard, E. J. Junior taking over for Dewey Mitchell at end, Allen Crumbley as the new right cornerback, and Ricky Tucker playing safety.

New men won jobs over returning starters in the kicking game, Woody Umphrey becoming the punter and Alan McElroy the placekicker. Tim Clark was kickoff man, Kevin Jones holder, and Barry Smith snapper.

Some backups had near first-team status, including Bruce Bolton at wide receiver, Billy Jackson at fullback, Curtis McGriff at noseguard, and Rickey Gilliland at linebacker.

The 1978 Alabama football team had a difficult schedule and found itself in a difficult situation in the opening game. Bama was hosting Nebraska at Legion Field in Birmingham and the

Cornhuskers—the only team to defeat Alabama in 1977—had a 3–0 lead. Nebraska had punted the Tide into a deep hole, inside the Alabama one yard line. On third and nine, fullback Billy Jackson ripped off a fourteen-yard run. That started what would be a ninety-nine-yard drive to a 7–3 lead en route to a 20–3 Alabama victory.

Tough schedules had become the norm for Bama. The 1977 national championship was the victim of a one-touchdown loss at Nebraska, and Alabama's other nonconference games were against Southern Cal, Miami, and Louisville. In 1978 it was tougher (because Miami and Louisville were not yet powers). After the opener against Nebraska, Alabama would go to Missouri (the Tigers had cost Alabama a chance at the 1975 national championship as Bama's only loss was 20–17 to Missouri in the season opener), host USC in Birmingham, have its Southeastern Conference opener against Vanderbilt, and then go to Washington. The other nonconference game would be against Virginia Tech (also not yet a power).

"Typically, Alabama teams got stronger as the year went along," said Major Ogilvie. "In 1978 we had to be pretty good from the get-go."

Mal Moore, who was offensive coordinator and quarterbacks coach for Alabama, said, "We never worried about a tough schedule. We thought we could beat anyone. We had good players, we worked hard, and we drew strength from Coach Bryant." After switching to the triple option offense in 1971, Alabama won an average of more than ten games per season.

The 1978 Alabama team was the popular pick as the preseason number-one team, including the most-recognized poll, that of the Associated Press.

It was blazing hot in Columbia when Alabama took on Missouri. It was an unusual game, Bama roaring out to a quick 17–0 lead. But the home team fought back on the strength of a long run, a long interception return for a touchdown (ending Rutledge's Alabama record streak of one hundred straight passes without an interception), and a short drive to take a 20–17 halftime lead.

The specifics of Bryant's halftime address to his team have remained secret, but there has been no lack of confirmation that it matched the blistering heat on the field. The challenge he gave his team would be considered a step on the road to the championship.

Early in the third quarter E. J. Junior blocked a punt, Rickey Gilliland caught it, and Gilliland ran it thirty-five yards for a go-ahead touchdown. Alabama cruised to a 38–20 win.

Although Alabama has a good all-time record against Southern Cal (5–2) and the Tide had suffered only one loss in five previous meetings prior to 1978, the game in Birmingham would not be a good one for Bama. Later Alabama critics would say the Trojans' 24–14 win was not as close as the final score. In truth, two plays may have made the difference in the outcome. In any event, number-one ranked Alabama was defeated and replaced at the top of the standings by USC. At that time a national championship seemed unlikely. Bama fell from first to seventh in the AP poll.

One aspect of the Bryant process was to be in position to take advantage of opportunities. Later in the season the Trojans were upset by Arizona State, convincingly, 20–7. That opened the door for Alabama to get back in the championship race. Over the years there have been any number of times that Alabama needed a certain circumstance to occur—a circumstance outside the control of Bama—in order for the Tide to have a chance. This was the first of several such circumstances in 1978.

One circumstance of Alabama schedules prior to 1992 was that Vanderbilt was always on the menu. Bama's 1978 team won by 51–28 in Tuscaloosa, but the game was not near as easy as that final score would make it appear. The Commodores led 21–16 in the third quarter in Tuscaloosa, but Tony Nathan gave the Tide the

lead for good with a sixty-three-yard run. Lou Ikner would add a
sixty-one-yard run in Bama's 27-point fourth quarter.

In 1975, Alabama had hosted Washington in celebration of the
fiftieth anniversary of the Crimson Tide team that had started
Bama's fabulous bowl tradition. The 1925 team had upset Washington, 20–19, in the 1926 Rose Bowl. A handful of surviving players on both teams, and Wallace Wade, who had been Alabama's
coach, attended a reunion in conjunction with the game.
The 1975 team didn't have near as much trouble with the Huskies as did that Rose Bowl squad. Alabama won 52–0.

The return game came as a part of that tough nonconference
schedule in 1978. Alabama went to Seattle to face a good Washington team featuring an outstanding wide receiver, Spider Gaines.
Gaines lived up to his billing by taking a first quarter pass seventy-eight yards for a touchdown.

The tough 20–17 win wasn't secured until Murray Legg recovered a fumble late in the fourth quarter. After the game many in
the Alabama camp felt the Tide had not only beaten a good Washington team but had overcome some curious officiating from the
Pac-Ten crew.

A statistical oddity following the win was that it gave Bryant
an overall coaching record of 277–77–16—200 more victories than
losses.

Alabama then started into the meat of its SEC schedule with a
23–12 win over Florida in Tuscaloosa. The Gators in Tuscaloosa
were rare in those days, but Florida did have the distinction of having posted the only victory over a Bryant-coached Bama team in
Alabama's stadium. That came in 1963. There wouldn't be another
Tuscaloosa loss for Alabama under Bryant until his final season.
(Most big home games in those days were played in larger Legion
Field in Birmingham.)

That weekend, Southern Cal was upset by Arizona State and

Bama moved to number three in the nation, behind Oklahoma and Penn State.

Alabama was dominating Tennessee in those days and the eighth-straight Bama win over the Vols wasn't as close as the final score. It was 30–3 at the end of three quarters. The Vols scored a meaningless touchdown in the final seconds to lose 30–17. Alabama had a couple of unusual touchdown plays in the game in Knoxville. Tight end Tim Travis scored on close-quarters end-around runs with Major Ogilvie throwing devastating blocks. On one of those plays Travis dropped the ball, but it bounced right back into his hands, and he never broke stride in going into the end zone.

That ended Alabama's road games for the year. The final four included a weak Virginia Tech team that Bama defeated 35–0 in Tuscaloosa and three games in Birmingham. Mississippi State was defeated 35–14, and LSU was steamrolled 31–10.

The win over the Bengal Tigers was not without merit. LSU was ranked tenth in the nation. But since switching to the wishbone in 1971, Alabama had lost a total of only three SEC games in eight years. Two of those losses came in 1976, the only season in that stretch Bama did not win the league championship.

LSU featured outstanding running back Charles Alexander and the Tigers took a 7–0 lead. But fueled by a fourth-down pass by punter Woody Umphrey and a defense that held Alexander to only forty-six yards on his fourteen carries, Bama won going away.

The same day, number-one ranked Oklahoma had fallen to ninth-ranked Nebraska, which moved to number two. Penn State was number one and Alabama number three.

Alabama then had an unusual schedule situation, two straight open weeks before the regular season finish against Auburn.

But just because Alabama wasn't playing for a couple of weeks didn't mean significant things weren't happening.

Alabama moved from third to second in the AP poll without

even playing. Bowl game invitations were issued on November 19, an open date for Alabama. Prior to games on November 18, Joe Paterno of number-one ranked Penn State had said that if number-two Nebraska defeated Missouri (as expected), the Nittany Lions would play the Cornhuskers in the Orange Bowl. And because Georgia was undefeated in SEC play, if the Bulldogs of Coach Vince Dooley could defeat Auburn (also as expected), an old SEC rule would send Georgia to New Orleans because Bama had been there more recently (the previous year against Ohio State).

A representative of the Cotton Bowl was in Tuscaloosa on that weekend when Alabama was not playing to issue an invitation to the Crimson Tide to come to Dallas and play Houston.

Almost as if Coach Bryant willed it, Missouri upset the Cornhuskers, 35–21. Early in the year, when the Tide was headed to Columbia, Bama had been concerned about Missouri's giant-killer reputation. In late November it was an appreciated upset.

Some Alabama fans would rather Bama not have a chance at the national championship than root for Auburn to win. Those fans could be satisfied with what the Tigers were able to accomplish against Georgia, a 22–22 tie. Those circumstances, presumably beyond Coach Bryant's control, set the stage for Alabama to have a chance at the national championship.

Some thought that Penn State's Paterno was pleased that those circumstances came about. He had no love for the Orange Bowl, which had misled him the year before. An Orange Bowl invitation that had been promised to the Lions instead went to Arkansas, and Penn State went to the Fiesta Bowl (a minor bowl in 1977). Additionally, Paterno had appreciated Bryant convincing the Sugar Bowl to take Penn State instead of the Big Eight runner-up to play against the 1975 Alabama team in New Orleans.

First, though, Alabama had to defeat Auburn. Prior to the game, Bryant said if Alabama did not defeat Auburn he didn't think Bama should go to any bowl game, and that would be his recommendation to the university. The Tide was aiming for its twentieth consecutive bowl game. In fact, had Bama lost to Auburn the Tide would have been consigned to the Bluebonnet Bowl.

The Tigers had a backfield of future NFL stars—Joe Cribbs, James Brooks, and William Andrews—and Auburn put up a battle for a half. Bama pulled away in the second half. Rutledge had two touchdown passes to Bruce Bolton and one to Rick Neal, and backup quarterback Steadman Shealy closed out the scoring with a twenty-yard run. It was Alabama's sixth-straight victory over the Tigers.

Bryant said, "If we have a chance, we want to play over our heads." There was only one team over Bama going into the bowls. In all polls it was Penn State number one and Alabama number two.

Henry Bodenheimer of the Sugar Bowl didn't mince words. "We want an Alabama–Penn State matchup," he said.

Field Scovell of the Cotton Bowl wanted Penn State, but he was realistic. "You don't tell number one what to do," Scovell said. "He does what he damn well pleases."

And so it was: the first match of number one versus number two since second-ranked Alabama had been clobbered by national champion Nebraska in the Orange Bowl at the conclusion of the 1971 season. (Many believe the Sugar Bowl at the end of the 1973 season was a one versus two. Alabama was number one, but Notre Dame was ranked third.)

Despite gaudy credentials, Penn State was looking for its first national championship. The Lions led the nation in defense and were also first in rushing defense, allowing a miserly 54.5 yards per game. It would be Penn State's first game against a wishbone team.

The Lions had six All-America players. Quarterback Chuck Fusina had received more first place votes for the Heisman Trophy than anyone, but finished second to Oklahoma's Billy Sims.

Tackles Bruce Clark and Matt Millen were considered the best tandem on one team in decades.

Bama had two All-America honorees, linebacker Barry Krauss and defensive tackle Marty Lyons.

Alabama's wishbone was more diverse than most. For one thing, Bama did more than just line up in a wishbone formation. Many teams were in the full house backfield, but ran called plays. Tide quarterbacks made split-second decisions based on what defenders did. The bread-and-butter triple-option play involved the quarterback first deciding if the defensive end was closing on the fullback. If he did not close, the fullback got the football. If the end closed, the quarterback pulled it back from the belly of the fullback and looked for the second option, which was a quarterback keeper. If a defender was in position to take the quarterback, he pitched to the halfback, who had another halfback leading interference for him. Alabama didn't have the speed of some other wishbone teams, but the halfbacks were excellent blockers.

And the Alabama wishbone used the pass. In fact, even though he was exclusively a wishbone quarterback in his Bama career, Jeff Rutledge broke Joe Namath's career touchdown passes record as Rutledge pitched for thirty.

During the year three teams ranked number one had been defeated: Alabama, Southern Cal, and Oklahoma. Behind the scenes, ABC approached the NCAA about the possibility of matching Alabama and Southern Cal in a post-bowl championship game if Bama defeated Penn State. The NCAA turned down the proposal, as well as an ABC request for overtime in the Sugar Bowl if necessary.

The forty-fifth Sugar Bowl was a game in which it seemed the outcome might turn on every play. Tension was as high as can be imagined. And there were a handful of plays that made the difference.

Just before halftime in a scoreless game, a couple of non-plays were important. Alabama was probably going to be content to run out the clock with just 1:11 to play, but Penn State twice called time out hoping to get the ball back. Instead, Tony Nathan ripped off runs of thirty and seven yards to the Penn State thirty. Rutledge then connected with Bolton in the end zone with only eight seconds to play in the first half. Alan McElroy kicked the extra point.

Penn State picked off a Rutledge pass in the third quarter and the Lions took advantage to tie the game. Fusina hit Penn State's fine wide receiver, Scott Fitzkee, deep in the end zone, and All-America place-kicker Matt Bahr tied the game at 7–7.

Later in the third quarter Lou Ikner returned a Penn State punt sixty-two yards to the Lions eleven yard line. Three plays later sophomore Major Ogilvie hammered in for the touchdown. (Ogilvie would end his career with an NCAA record, scoring touchdowns in four bowl games.)

Almost no one remembers the scoring, though. It was the non-score.

With just under eight minutes to play, Alabama lost a pitchout, and Penn State was set up at the Alabama nineteen.

The Lions moved to a first down inside the 10. A rush got nothing, then Fusina hit Fitzkee near the end zone. Don McNeal said, "I was covering someone else, but I saw the pass was going to Fitzkee and broke on the ball. (Murray Legg had slipped down.) I didn't have time to think. It was just instinct. I knew I had to make a perfect tackle or Fitzkee would fall into the end zone." The perfect tackle set up the dramatic finish.

Penn State had two excellent backs, Matt Suhey and Mike Guman. Suhey got the first opportunity and was slammed down inside the one yard line. Guman was called on next.

Linebacker Barry Krauss said, "We had just stopped a dive play, and I thought they would probably play action or sweep. But Coach Donahue (Bama defensive coordinator Ken Donahue) made a great call for us to sell out and crash the corners. The defensive line did an incredible job of reestablishing the line of scrimmage.

"So, yes, he went over the top, and I was the one who hit him. But that was because of what the defensive line had done. It was Coach Bryant's plan that the defensive line would take out the interference and let the linebackers make the play. And then Murray came in and pushed us back, keeping the back from twisting and maybe falling into the end zone. Everyone was involved. It was the epitome of Alabama defense, which was teamwork at its best."

In the dressing room it was obvious Tide players had given all. It was as subdued as a losers' locker room. Krauss was selected MVP, his second bowl MVP award as he had also won the honor in the Liberty Bowl at the end of the 1976 season.

Bryant said, "It was the finest defensive effort I can recall. It was the most critical series I can remember."

Then it was time for the poll bowl. Alabama had been denied in poll voting enough times to be skittish, but when number two beats number one head-to-head, it would seem to be obvious. And it was in the Associated Press voting and in selections by the Football Writers' Association of America for the MacArthur Bowl and by the National Football Foundation. Alabama was a solid number one.

Almost inexplicably—particularly since Southern Cal's Rose Bowl win had come via an obvious official's error—the United Press International vote of coaches had USC number one and Bama number two. (The two had an equal number of first-place votes, but the Trojans had more second-place votes.)

"That's the first time I can remember that the writers were much more knowledgeable than the coaches," Bryant said.

# TABLE 10

## 1978

Coach Paul W. "Bear" Bryant

AP National Champions, SEC Champions

Won 11, Lost 1

| Alabama | Opponent | | Location | Date |
|---|---|---|---|---|
| 20 | Nebraska | 3 | Birmingham | Sept. 2 |
| 38 | Missouri | 20 | Columbia | Sept. 16 |
| 14 | Southern Cal | 24 | Birmingham (TV) | Sept. 23 |
| 51 | Vanderbilt | 28 | Tuscaloosa | Sept. 30 |
| 20 | Washington | 17 | Seattle | Oct. 7 |
| 23 | Florida | 12 | Tuscaloosa | Oct. 14 |
| 30 | Tennessee | 17 | Knoxville | Oct. 21 |
| 35 | Virginia Tech | 0 | Tuscaloosa | Oct. 28 |
| 35 | Miss. State | 14 | Birmingham | Nov. 4 |
| 31 | LSU | 10 | Birmingham (TV) | Nov. 11 |
| 34 | Auburn | 16 | Birmingham | Dec. 2 |
| 14 | Penn State | 7 | Sugar Bowl (TV) | Jan. 1, 1979 |
| 345 | | 168 | | |

CHAPTER ELEVEN

# 1979

## Steve Townsend

**A**s the sun began its descent in
the western Birmingham sky on a late autumn afternoon in 1979,
the Crimson Tide quarterback Steadman Shealy looked up at the
Legion Field scoreboard to check the time left in the fourth quarter
of the Auburn game.

For the first time all year, Alabama trailed late in a game and
with just over eight minutes to play, the Crimson Tide had eighty-
two yards to travel in order to reclaim the lead and remain in the
national championship hunt. Huddled near the south end zone,
Shealy remembered getting goose bumps down his spine, "I said
this is do or die. That was the toughest situation I'd ever been in on
the football field."

With a Sugar Bowl bid and a number-one ranking on the line, the
Crimson Tide displayed the iron resolution of its coach, Paul Bryant,
to win the fourth quarter. On the final drive of the decade, the senior
quarterback from Dothan precisely marched the Tide to a touchdown and a 2-point conversion, giving Alabama a 25–18 victory, setting up yet another matchup for a national championship.

It was a special time to be an Alabama fan. Always a contender
and rarely a pretender, the Paul "Bear" Bryant teams of that era
were so unrelenting with its wishbone offense and so fierce defensively with the "Redwood Forest" the Crimson Tide rolled to the
title as the "Team of the Decade."

And, no team at any time in the history of the Southeastern

Major Ogilvie turns the corner on the triple-option play.

Conference matched such a relentless offensive machine with a suffocating defense that is often overlooked in the folklore of Crimson
Tide history.

"I played in 1961 and helped coached the 1979 and 1992 defenses," says Bill "Brother" Oliver. "I've been asked the great question of which was the best. I can tell you this; there has never been

a defense any better than 1979. I think that defense along with the '92 team are as good as you'll ever see in college football.

"The biggest difference in those two teams was we had a better offensive team in '79, but I'll tell you this. There has never been a defensive team that loved to play more than that '79 bunch. They loved to punish you from the first play to the last one. Nobody wanted any part of us. I guarantee you that."

The season started at Grant Field in Atlanta in a nationally televised game against Georgia Tech, a team that featured Pepper Rodgers as head coach and Steve Spurrier as the offensive coordinator.

"I was so in awe of Coach Bryant that I wanted to go over to him and sing, 'Yea, Alabama,'" remembered the effervescent Rodgers. "I really and truly wanted to go over and get Coach Bryant's autograph. I just didn't have enough guts to do it."

It was an era when a team could be on TV only five times over a two-year period, so the Yellow Jacket contest would be only one of two regular-season games that displayed live and in color the talents of this squad to viewing audiences.

With more than 30,000 Alabama fans cramped into a capacity crowd of 57,000, the Crimson Tide began defense of its national championship with a most impressive performance, winning 30–6.

At the end of the first quarter, All-American defensive end E. J. Junior intercepted a Mike Kelly pass and followed a blocking brigade of Bryon Braggs, Wayne Hamilton, and Randy Scott down the field for the first TD of the '79 season. "It was pretty easy," said Junior. "All I had to do was run because those guys just bowled over the would-be tacklers."

Shealy engineered the wishbone to perfection with Major Ogilvie, Steve Whitman, and Billy Jackson scoring touchdowns. The only disappointment was losing the shutout on the final play of the game.

"That touchdown on the final play of the game really hurt," said behemoth defensive lineman Braggs. "Our defense was planning on eating us some goose eggs for breakfast on Sunday. The first-team defense was on the bench and then I saw those yellow and white pompons and the Tech band playing the 'Ramblin' Wreck' song and I knew they'd scored."

Despite the last second TD, Jacket coach Pepper Rodgers was quick to praise the Tide in the postgame conversations. "I mean come on, their defense is unbelievable," said Rodgers. "I didn't think anyone could shut us down like that. They intimidated us, completely intimidated us."

In describing the game for the *Atlanta Constitution,* even long-time Coach Bryant and Alabama nemesis Furman Bisher was overwhelmed by what he saw. Writing in his Sunday column, Bisher duly noted, "You should be reminded Tech was playing a defense that plays like it is a mortal sin to give up a point."

A week later against a Baylor team that had just beaten Texas A&M and that had closed the '78 season with a 38–14 romp over Texas arrived at Legion Field in Birmingham with a 2–0 record and high hopes of an upset over the Crimson Tide.

"From watching Baylor film, I thought we'd be lucky to score seventeen points on a defense that featured Mike Singletary," remembered star running back Ogilvie.

By the end of the sultry September night, Alabama would have 45 points to zero for the Golden Bears in a display of football that even had the usually stoic Bryant to hint this team had the making of being very special.

Offensively, the Tide had rolled up twenty-four first downs and nearly 450 yards while holding Baylor to six first downs. Cornerback Don McNeal graded 100 percent for his efforts, charging Bryant to check back on his previous charts to determine that it was the first time since the days of Lee Roy Jordan that a defender had been perfect.

Six different Alabama defenders intercepted passes. There were six sacks as well, and future Hall of Fame coach Grant Teaff came away with the following remark, "In all my years of coaching, this is the best defensive team I've coached against and that includes some great ones at Texas and Penn State."

The Crimson Tide line had so battered the Baylor defense that tackle Jim Bunch earned the SEC Player of the Week honors for his offensive play.

After the thrashing of Baylor, the roll to number one continued with a 66–3 rout of Vanderbilt in Nashville and a 38–0 white-washing of Wichita State. As evidenced by the final scores, neither outcome was ever in doubt, but the final margins of victories could have been much worse if not for the benevolence of Paul Bryant.

"Coach Bryant had a genuine affection for Vanderbilt dating back to his days as an assistant coach there," remembered Kirk McNair, then the SID for the fabled Bama coach. "He never liked embarrassing anyone, especially Vandy."

The Commodore statistical crew had to work overtime sorting out the fourteen different Crimson Tide runners who carried the ball and the thirty different defenders who were credited with at least one tackle.

Vanderbilt coach George MacIntyre joined the growing list of admirers of this team. "I've seen a lot of great teams and I can honestly say I don't think I've ever witnessed a better football team in my career."

Wichita State was a late addition to the schedule in 1979, with the Shockers assuming the spot that was originally slated for national power SMU. The Ponies backed out of their contract and Coach Bryant's chief administrator Sam Bailey lined up the game with the outmanned Shockers from Kansas.

Despite its impressive 4–0 start, the Crimson Tide remained second in the polls behind Southern California. Next up was a trip to "The Swamp" in Gainesville where Alabama faced a Florida team coached by former Tide player Charley Pell.

There have been few more crushing days than this one in any

school's history. Even the final 40–0 score didn't indicate the sheer dominance and power of the relentless Crimson Tide this day.

"Today, Alabama was the most superior football team I've ever seen," said Pell in the aftermath of the demolition. For the game, the wishbone rolled up 22 first downs to the Gators' three. The Crimson Tide totaled 454 yards to Florida's 66.

Only once the whole afternoon did the Gators cross the midfield stripe and on the next play a swarm of white jerseys dropped Florida running back Terry Williams for a three-yard loss.

When top-ranked Southern California played to a tie with Stanford, Alabama climbed to number one for the first time, but despite the carnage left in Gainesville, the Tide flew back home a battered and bruised team.

"I never saw a team that good for the first half of the season," said longtime trainer Jim Goostree. "We just had a lot of injuries in Gainesville. On the plane back, Coach Bryant told me he didn't need an injury report because all he had to do was look around and see all the limping players."

## THE COMEBACK

If there was ever a game that symbolized the Paul Bryant era, it was on "this crystal blue autumn afternoon in Birmingham, Alabama, and a fine day for football on the third Saturday in October"—as legendary radio voice of the Tide John Forney described it.

The blue skies quickly turned into an orange blur as Tennessee used two turnovers and a short field to stun Alabama and take a 17–0 lead early in the second quarter. By his own admission, QB Shealy was having "the worst day of my career" and Bryant inserted his backup Don Jacobs to try to energize the slumping offense. When Jacobs lost a fumble on the Tennessee twenty-seven, the orange-clad Volunteer fans and players really were whipped into a frenzy and the quest for the national title seemed a dim memory.

"It was time we showed Tennessee some Alabama football," remembered defensive tackle Bryon Braggs. Volunteer quarterback Jimmy Streater, known as the "Silver Streak" was being chased by the front line of Braggs, David Hannah, and Warren Lyles when his pass was tipped by Lyles and intercepted by linebacker Robbie Jones.

A thirty-three-yard touchdown strike from Shealy to tight end Tim Travis cut the lead to 17–7. On the final play of the first half, freshman safety Tommy Wilcox knocked Streater down twelve yards behind the line of scrimmage, ending the half on a positive note.

Coach Bryant's halftime talk to the team is just one of the many things that made him a legend and separated him from his peers. "I was scared to death of what he was going to say at half," remembered Braggs. "When he said we have them right where we want them, I'd thought the man had lost it. He then talked about character and how we'd respond like champions."

And, the team did. On its first two possessions of the second half, the Tide scored with Ogilvie powering in from the six and the one. In the fourth quarter, Jacobs marched the Tide eighty yards and scored the game-clincher on a thirteen-yard run.

As the fourth-quarter clock wound down, Alabama methodically and systematically paraded down the field again, but the Tide let the clock run out with the ball within the shadows of the Tennessee goalpost. The final was 27–17 and as the overflow crowd of 77,000-plus exited historic Legion Field, the aroma of smoke from the victory cigars wafted into the Birmingham air.

It should be duly noted for historical purposes this was the first Alabama game ever televised on ESPN, though on a delayed basis because of the strict restrictions of the NCAA on TV in that era.

## HOPE AND DOGS

Appropriately, the theme for Homecoming '79 was "Stars Fell on Alabama," and it featured an appearance by Bob Hope on campus to film a special skit for NBC with Coach Bryant and Joe Namath.

Alabama's 31–7 victory over Virginia Tech seemed secondary to the appearance of Hope, who visited with Bryant in his office before they descended downstairs in Memorial Coliseum to the A-Club Room. Due to a plane delay, Namath was late to the shoot and when he entered the room, Hope quizzed him, "Have you read your lines, Joe?" Namath laughed and pointed to the script in his back pocket.

Bryant asked Hope, "Why didn't you ask me if I'd learned my lines, Bob?"

"I was too scared of you to ask," quipped Hope, which brought a round of laughs.

On the playing field there were more wounded stars on the sidelines than on the field, including halfback Major Ogilvie and receiver Keith Pugh, increasing the angst for the stretch drive against Mississippi State, LSU, Miami, and Auburn.

Emory Bellard brought the original wishbone attack to Starkville in 1979 and his Bulldogs employed a clock-churning version of the 'bone that kept Alabama's battered and bruised offense on the sidelines for much of the first half.

Quarterback Shealy, with most of his weapons sidelined with injuries, charged the Bama battery in the second half in a 24–7 workman-like victory. For the afternoon, the senior from Dothan rushed for a QB running record of 190 yards.

In winning 21 straight SEC games, Alabama eclipsed a record set by General Robert Neyland's Tennessee teams. Bellard was quick to praise the Alabama coach afterward. "Alabama's talent level is really no better than ours and certainly not Tennessee's or

LSU's, but the difference is the man on the sidelines. Alabama is a great team because they are mentally tougher and do the little things better than the rest of us. They are champions because they believe they are and that's because of the man in the houndstooth hat.' "

## RAINDROPS FALL IN BATON ROUGE

The old adage that it never rains in Tiger Stadium proved to be totally false when a deluge of the wet stuff cascaded from the Baton Rouge skies on to the soaked grass surface.

Escaping with a 3–0 victory, thanks to a third quarter field goal by Alan McElroy, was just one of the prayers answered that inclement weekend. Just getting to Baton Rouge proved challenging enough, as the team plane rocked under thunder jolts and lightning flashed by the windows.

"I wasn't even supposed to make the trip," remembered Ogilvie, who had been hurt and sidelined for two weeks. "Coach Goostree was giving me special treatments all week and Coach Bryant told me at Friday's workout in Tuscaloosa that he wanted me to go with the team for moral support.

"I was catching punts in pregame warmups and Coach Goostree came up to me and asked me how I was feeling. I told him I felt better and he said, 'Good, because Coach Bryant just told me to tell you that you are starting tonight.'"

On the first play from scrimmage, Ogilvie carried left on the option and barreled for a six-yard gain before he was rolled out of bounds. "I just popped up and ran back for the second play, and I was feeling pretty good. The next day I learned I had clipped Coach Bryant and sent him sprawling."

On his TV show, Coach Bryant laughed and said, "That was the only good block Major made all night long."

Despite the 3–0 score, Alabama totally dominated the game
with LSU crossing midfield only once. The wet ball did lessen the
wishbone's effectiveness and Bryant was happy to get out of town
with a win, noting "all they needed was for one of our secondary
men to fall down on a long pass play."

LSU's Charlie McClendon was most impressed by what he saw,
especially by the Redwood Forest defense. "We've played both USC
and Alabama, and I'd take Alabama because of that defense. Fel-
las, that is the best defensive team I've ever seen."

The next weekend Alabama posted its sixth shutout of the year,
beating Miami 30–0 in the first-ever televised game from Tuscaloosa. Howard Schnellenberger's Hurricanes were coming off a
win over Penn State, but even Hall of Fame quarterback Jim Kelly
couldn't find any gaps in the Tide defense, one that pilfered five
passes, knocked down eight others, and sacked the respective QBs
five more times.

When Alabama staged its fourth-quarter comeback two weeks
later versus Auburn on December 1, there were no doubters in crimson. "I had the greatest feeling in the world," said All-American
tackle Jim Bunch. "We had prepared all our careers for a fourth-
quarter drive and we weren't going to be denied."

"We should have won the game 24–3," said quarterback Shealy,
"but we fumbled five times in the second half and gave them two
touchdowns. We actually fumbled on the first play of the winning
drive. Fortunately, Major Ogilvie recovered it. I think it was the
biggest play of the game."

Shealy ripped off gains of nine, fifteen, and two before hitting Keith Pugh on a pass play that pushed the ball to Auburn's
twenty-eight. Steve Whitman ripped through a gaping hole to the
Tiger eight and a play later Shealy danced past Auburn defenders
for a TD and a subsequent 2-point conversion.

Beating Auburn was a challenge; especially since the Tiger offense featured the running back duo of Joe Cribbs and James

Brooks, the first-ever tandem to rush for more than 1,000 yards apiece.

"I've seen better games but I've never seen a better drive to win a game," said Coach Bryant after the win.

Despite the victory, Alabama tumbled to number two in the polls behind Ohio State. "I'm not worried about polls, just Arkansas," was the terse reminder from the Alabama coach as the Tide prepared for a Sugar Bowl showdown with the Razorbacks.

On the first day of 1980, Alabama sealed its right as the "Team of the Decade" for the 1970s with a convincing 24–9 victory over Lou Holtz's Arkansas team. Ogilvie scored two touchdowns, and Steve Whitman raced through a gaping hole provided by All-American center Dwight Stephenson to score the final on an eleven-yard run that capped a ninety-eight-yard drive in the fourth quarter.

Interceptions by Jim Bob Harris and Tommy Wilcox along with a devastating performance by the defensive front, anchored by E. J. Junior, Wayne Hamilton, Byron Braggs, and Randy Scott, mauled the Razorback offense just like they had their previous eleven opponents.

Later that New Year's Day, number-one Ohio State fell to Southern Cal in the Rose Bowl, delivering a unanimous national championship to the Crimson Tide, prompting Braggs to brag, "The only feeling better than playing for the national title in New Orleans on January 1 is being in Tuscaloosa on January 2 to celebrate winning it."

Jim Bunch, Dwight Stephenson, and Don McNeal earned All-American honors for the national champs while linebacker Thomas Boyd, tackle Braggs, guard Mike Brock, tackle David Hannah, safety Jim Bob Harris, end E. J. Junior, halfback Ogilvie, and quarterback Shealy joined them on the first-team All-SEC squad.

For the year, the Crimson Tide averaged keeping the ball thirty-six minutes a game, had eighteen different players rush the football and eighteen score points, fourteen different players intercepted a pass, and ten different ones recovered at least one fumble.

Most important, it was the sixth overall national title for Coach Bryant, and the fifth consensus championship, still a national record.

## TABLE 11

### 1979

Coach Paul W. "Bear" Bryant

AP & UPI National Champions, SEC Champions

Won 12, Lost 0

| Alabama | Opponent | | Location | Date |
|---|---|---|---|---|
| 30 | Georgia Tech | 6 | Atlanta (TV) | Sept. 8 |
| 45 | Baylor | 0 | Birmingham (N) | Sept. 22 |
| 66 | Vanderbilt | 3 | Nashville | Sept. 29 |
| 38 | Wichita State | 0 | Tuscaloosa | Oct. 6 |
| 40 | Florida | 0 | Gainesville | Oct. 13 |
| 27 | Tennessee | 17 | Birmingham | Oct. 20 |
| 31 | Virginia Tech | 7 | Tuscaloosa | Oct. 27 |
| 24 | Miss. State | 7 | Tuscaloosa | Nov. 3 |
| 3 | LSU | 0 | Baton Rouge (N) | Nov. 10 |
| 30 | Miami (Fla.) | 0 | Tuscaloosa (TV) | Nov. 17 |
| 25 | Auburn | 18 | Birmingham | Dec. 1 |
| 24 | Arkansas | 9 | Sugar Bowl (TV) | Jan. 1, 1980 |
| 383 | | 67 | | |

## CHAPTER TWELVE

# 1992

## GENE STALLINGS WITH ERIK STINNETT

Thirteen wins. Zero losses. That 1992 squad I coached was the only 13–0 team Alabama has ever had.

That may be because they're the only one that played thirteen games, I don't know. So I would think that team could play with any of Alabama's other national championship teams. I do know this: That 1992 team was a good team, an outstanding defensive team that could run the football. It was also a team that stayed relatively injury-free. That sort of combination is hard to beat.

The results showed on the field. We beat every team on our schedule.

But that was also the first year for the SEC championship game, giving us one extra game on our schedule. We had won our division, but basically we still hadn't won anything. We were 11–0 and we had to play Florida in the championship game. Well, we beat Florida 28–21 with Antonio Langham making the big interception right near the latter part of the game where he took it in for the touchdown. For some reason, I felt that if we hadn't played that championship game we may not have had the opportunity to play Miami for the national championship. Now, we were 12–0, but we still hadn't won anything other than the Southeastern Conference.

In our preparations for Miami, our confidence was high, but our confidence level was always at a high anyway. If you go 12–0 in this

George Teague celebrates a touchdown following his interception of a Miami pass.

conference, you're not lacking confidence. We had won twenty-two games in a row, and it wasn't like we hadn't played against good football teams. At that time, we led the nation in three or four categories defensively. The name of the game defensively is points, and we had given up fewer points, fewer rushing yards, fewer passing yards, fewer total yards than just about anyone, so I knew we could contain Miami.

On top of that, I knew we could run the football, and if you can run the football and you can stop the run, you've got a chance to win the game. So I really felt like we were the best football team. Now, no one would listen to me. Every time I did a press conference or something of that nature, I would say that I felt like we had the best football team. Sure, Miami had a better won-loss record over a three-year period than we did, they had some national champion-ship teams, and they deserved to be right where they were. I'm not saying that we should have been picked as the favorite. I'm just say-ing that I personally felt like we had the best football team.

The media, of course, didn't agree with me. But the media doesn't play. If you listen to the people in the stands or if you listen to the media too much, you'll be sitting with them and become a part of them. What does the media know? How many teams have they ever got ready to play? So I wasn't concerned about what oth-ers thought.

I also wasn't concerned with what Miami players thought. From the strut they had in their walk and the comments you read in the paper, I thought that they felt like they had the greater speed. They did have outstanding team speed, but we had good speed, too.

We respected Miami. But intimidated by them? No. Why would we be intimidated when we played teams like Florida, Auburn, Tennessee, and LSU? We played in a tough conference. Just be-cause it was Miami, that was not an intimidation factor for our team at all. In fact, they would probably be as intimidated as we were even though they were coming off a national championship season.

I know as the head coach I certainly wasn't intimidated, but, then again, I've never lacked in confidence. I've been a captain on just about every team I've ever played on, and I was captain of the football team at Texas A&M. I loved to play, and I loved to compete. Plus, you have to remember, I was exposed to Coach Paul Bryant both as a player and as a coach, and I was exposed to Coach Tom Landry for fourteen years. Those are the two best. Coach Landry was the best in pro ball, and Coach Bryant was the best in college ball. So I was well schooled. When I came to Alabama, all I needed to do was put together a good coaching staff, recruit some good players and sort of keep them in position. And that's what I did. I didn't have to build the team up every week. The team just needed to play up to its capabilities. You win games with football players making plays; you don't win with schemes.

That's how we won in '92.

But once we made it to the Sugar Bowl that season, I knew I needed to be careful with how I handled our players. I didn't want to put too much emphasis on the game. I knew the stakes were high. But if I put too much emphasis on it, I felt like I would have the players uptight, and I didn't want that. It was another game, the next game on the schedule, and I always felt like your last game ought to be your best game. We had beaten Florida the game before, and we had beaten Auburn the game before that, so it wasn't like we weren't already playing pretty good.

As it turned out, the players responded well to the way we went about our business in New Orleans. We practiced well, and the guys behaved themselves. I was extremely proud of the way they acted and conducted themselves. You know, you could have taken twenty preachers to New Orleans and they wouldn't have acted any nicer than our guys did. I've said this a number of times regarding that particular game: We took our entire squad—one hundred and some odd people—to New Orleans, and we did not have one person late for curfew. Miami moved their team out of their hotel the night before the game, but I left my team right where they were, and we were kind of in the middle of the French Quarter. You say, 'What's that got to do with it?' The thing was, our players were there to play a game. We weren't there on vacation. I received a little bit of criticism from people who felt like I should have moved them, but I thought that would be more of a hassle than leaving them where they were.

As for our game plan against Miami, first, we wanted to run the football offensively. Second, we wanted to confuse Gino Torretta, their Heisman-Trophy-winning quarterback, defensively, which would include putting eleven men up on the line from time to time.

It was as simple as that. It wasn't a matter of having to challenge our players. They didn't need to be challenged. I love the competitor, and the players we had on that '92 team were competitors.

Once the game began, we went about executing our game plan, and everything seemed to work. The fact we were controlling the line of scrimmage defensively was big. They had been averaging several hundred yards of offense a game, and we were holding them to three-and-outs. So they were the ones losing their confidence, not us.

We were ahead 13–6 at halftime, but, I have to admit, I felt a little uptight. Sure, I'd rather be up 13–6 than down 13–6, but as far as feeling good, I really didn't feel good. We were playing pretty well, but the first five minutes of the second half usually determines the result of the game, and we still had that to play.

Well, the first five minutes of the second half went our way. Tommy Johnson intercepted a pass that led to a touchdown, and then right after that George Teague intercepted another pass that he returned for a score. All of a sudden, we went from being up 13–6 to up 27–6. Those were two great defensive plays right there that sort of set the tempo for the second half. But I had been in games where the opponent had come back, and Miami had such great team speed, and they had come back time after time.

Then Teague made that unbelievable play where he chased down Lamar Thomas from behind, stole the ball from him, and started running back the other direction. Of course, my first reaction was that if Teague had been covering his man like he was supposed to, he wouldn't have had to make that great play. As it turned out, that was probably one of the greatest individual plays I've ever seen. Tyrone Prothro's catch on the defender's back was a great individual play, too. But Teague's play came in a big game.

Even after that, I still didn't feel like the game was over, and it wasn't over. Miami ran back a punt for a touchdown to make it 27–13, and with half of the fourth quarter still to play, the outcome was still undecided. That's when we faced a fourth-and-inches at midfield. We went for it, and fullback Martin Houston gained two yards for the first down. We went on to score a touchdown to make it 34–13 with just a few minutes to play.

If we hadn't converted on that fourth down, it would have been a very bad decision. In fact, when you look back over it, probably the smart thing to do would have been to punt the ball. But I also knew if we could make that first down and sustain the ball a little bit longer, we could run more clock. That's why I made the decision. Was it a good decision? Probably not. As good a defense as we had, it probably would have been wiser to punt the ball and make them go eighty or ninety yards with the football.

Despite being ahead by 21 points, I didn't feel good about the game until about a minute and a half before it was over. That's when I felt like we were going to win it. As the final seconds ticked off the clock, the players surprised me with a Gatorade bath and then hoisted me up on their shoulders and carried me to midfield. That was a little bit embarrassing, because the game's not for the coaches, it's for the players. If I was strong enough, I would have carried all of them off, but I wasn't strong enough.

In the locker room afterward, we did basically the same thing we did after every other game. We always had a prayer—not involving whether we won or lost but concerning the fact that we escaped the game without injury. Then we all hugged one another. We had the trophy in there, and I was extremely proud of our players.

The entire coaching staff had come up with an excellent game plan for that contest, and even though schemes don't win games, our players did a good job of handling their responsibilities and carrying out the game plan. We intercepted some passes, made some outstanding defensive plays, and put pressure on the quarterback, and the rest is history.

I was so pleased for the players. They hung in there after we started off my first season 0–3. We went from 0–3 in 1990 to winning the national championship two years later. Then again Alabama fans expect Alabama to win the national championship about every eight or nine years, and it had been thirteen years since the last one. So it was our time.

## TABLE 12

### 1992

Coach Gene Stallings

Unanimous National Champions, SEC Champions

Won 13, Lost 0

| Alabama | Opponent | | Location | Date |
|---------|----------|---|----------|------|
| 25 | Vanderbilt | 8 | Tuscaloosa (TV) | Sept. 5 |
| 17 | Southern Miss | 10 | Birmingham | Sept. 12 |
| 38 | Arkansas | 11 | Little Rock (N) | Sept. 19 |
| 13 | Louisiana Tech | 0 | Birmingham | Sept. 26 |
| 48 | South Carolina | 7 | Tuscaloosa | Oct. 3 |
| 37 | Tulane | 0 | New Orleans (N) | Oct. 10 |
| 17 | Tennessee | 10 | Knoxville (TV) | Oct. 17 |
| 31 | Ole Miss | 10 | Tuscaloosa | Oct. 24 |
| 31 | LSU | 11 | Baton Rouge (TV) | Nov. 7 |
| 30 | Miss. State | 21 | Starkville (N,TV) | Nov. 14 |
| 17 | Auburn | 0 | Birmingham (TV) | Nov. 26 |
| 28 | Florida | 21 | Birmingham (TV) | Dec. 5 |
| 34 | Miami | 13 | Sugar Bowl (N,TV) | Jan. 1, 1993 |
| 366 | | 122 | | |

## CHAPTER THIRTEEN

# 2009

## Eryk Anders, Javier Arenas, and Tommy Deas

The tale of Alabama's 2009 national championship season had its beginnings at the end of the previous campaign. The Crimson Tide had gone a long while without a national title, since 1992, and had gone through many ups and downs in the years since.

Alabama turned to head coach Nick Saban in 2007, hiring him away from the Miami Dolphins of the National Football League to bring him back to the college ranks where he had won a national championship at LSU. Before that, he built Michigan State into a respectable power. Alabama won six of its first eight games in Saban's first season, but nosedived to lose four in a row before finishing with an Independence Bowl victory over Colorado. Few had reason to believe that 2008 would be a big year for Alabama, but an injection of talent from a recruiting class that had brought in freshmen like Julio Jones, Mark Ingram, and Dont'a Hightower fueled a quick turnaround.

Alabama went undefeated in the regular season, rising to number one in the national rankings, and had only to beat second-ranked Florida in the SEC Championship Game to play for a national title. The Crimson Tide led by a field goal going into the fourth quarter, but fell 31–21, a defeat that was crushing to players who had been hopeful of winning it all. That demoralization carried over into the

Marcell Dareus evades the Texas quarterback on his way to the end zone, photograph by Kent Gidley.

Sugar Bowl, where an unmotivated Alabama team lost to Utah. A season with so much promise had ended in a flameout.

But it also ignited a fire. "It left a really bad taste in our mouths," says Eryk Anders, a linebacker from San Antonio who was a senior on the 2009 team. "We didn't lose that many seniors, we had a lot of returning players who remembered what it felt like. It was definitely, at the time, something I wish didn't happen, but in retrospect maybe it was a good thing that it did happen. The years before that a lot of people worked hard, but after that *everybody* worked hard. Everybody went above and beyond."

Saban had one message for the team coming off the bowl loss: forget about it. "After the Utah loss the previous season, Coach Saban told us to put all that behind us," says Javier Arenas, a senior cornerback in 2009. "It helped us mature. The guys who were seniors the next year, and even the juniors, we learned a lot from that."

Before the first snap of the season, Alabama players felt rejuvenated and confident. They were ready to make another run. "We were fresh," Arenas says. "We felt how good we were going to be going through offseason training."

The quest to try to finish the mission that was unfulfilled in the previous season began where the last season unraveled. Alabama—ranked number five in the Associated Press preseason poll, coming off the 12–2 finish from the year before—played seventh-ranked Virginia Tech in the 2009 season opener in the Georgia Dome in Atlanta in the Chick-fil-A Kickoff Game. In a game that would serve as a model for the season's success, albeit one that was far from error-free, Alabama dominated late by scoring eighteen points in the final twelve minutes and twenty-three seconds to win 34–24. Ingram—the sophomore running back from Flint, Michigan—rushed for 150 yards on twetnty-six carries, scoring on a six-yard run and an eighteen-yard reception. Dependable Leigh Tiffin kicked four field goals.

The Tide didn't return to campus satisfied with a ten-point victory. "From my perspective, and I was a captain on the team, it was an OK game," Arenas says. "We won pretty big, but I still didn't see us going undefeated. I knew we were capable of it, but I knew we had a lot of work to do from there."

Alabama had talent and coaching, but would need another crucial element, leadership. "Guys really stepped up. There was kind of a baptism by fire with guys like Rolando McClain and Javier Arenas," said Anders, referring to the inside linebacker and cornerback who took on key roles in leading the defense. "Everybody had to fill their role on the team, whether it was in a leadership role or supporting cast, special teams—everybody did their job."

On offense, an unheralded quarterback named Greg McElroy came into his own, embracing Saban's first-do-no-harm philosophy by avoiding turnovers while making plays in key moments. He completed fifteen of thirty attempts for 230 yards and a touchdown in the opener, and would become more efficient as the season progressed. "He played a huge part, "Arenas says. "He did what he was supposed to do. He didn't step out and try to be Superman. The quarterback isn't bigger than the team, and Greg fit that role perfectly."

After the victory over a top-ten opponent to open the season, Alabama went on a roll and began to climb in the rankings. Following out-of-conference home wins over Florida International (40–14) and North Texas (53–7), Alabama crushed Arkansas (35–7) in Bryant-Denny Stadium. They then went on the road to handle Kentucky (38–20) and Ole Miss (22–3). The Tide returned home to beat South Carolina (20–6).

Alabama football in the twenty-first century, as the Crimson Tide made its way through the 2009 season, greatly resembled the model patented by Wallace Wade, Frank Thomas, Paul W. "Bear" Bryant, and Gene Stallings in engineering championship seasons at the Capstone: strong defense and a physical running game with a devotion to avoiding mistakes that might hand a game to the opposing team. Alabama didn't defeat teams with flash as much as it beat them into submission.

Along the way, a star emerged. Ingram, sometimes taking direct snaps while operating out of the wildcat formation, stepped to the front to lead a stable of runners that also included rising star Trent Richardson and seasoned veteran Roy Upchurch. Ingram rambled for 140 yards and two touchdowns on twenty-two carries at Kentucky. Then he torched Ole Miss for 172 yards on twenty-eight carries, and took the team on his shoulders to trample South Carolina to the tune of 246 yards on twenty-four attempts.

As the Crimson Tide forged an offensive identity, it also molded a dominant unit on the other side of the ball. After the opener, Alabama allowed more than fifteen points to an opponent just once (to Kentucky) until the final week of the regular season. Alabama battered opposing quarterbacks and ball-hawked its way to turnovers.

The defense knew it was good, but didn't dwell on it. "We kind of just took it a game at a time," Anders says. "I don't think we ever looked past anybody, and we never stood back and admired our work. We never said, 'We held Darren McFadden to forty yards,' or we stopped this quarterback or this running back. It was, OK, we won that game, let's correct our mistakes and get ready for the next game."

The next game after the stretch of four SEC wins turned out to be the most difficult of Alabama's season. Unheralded Tennessee marched into Tuscaloosa with a modest 3–3 record under a brash, young first-year head coach named Lane Kiffin (who later added to Alabama's championship tradition as offensive coordinator under Saban) to face a Crimson Tide team that had risen to the number one spot in the national ranking. But there were other dynamics at work. For one, it was a rivalry game. For another, Alabama was playing for the eighth week in a row, and its own brand of physical football was taking a toll on its players. The Volunteers, on the other hand, had fresh legs coming off an open date. "We were very tired," Arenas says.

Alabama looked listless. Tennessee couldn't muster much against the stonewall defense, but the Crimson Tide struggled. Even so, Alabama seemed to have things in hand. They were up 12–3 with the ball as the clock ran under four minutes in the fourth quarter. But Ingram, who was held to ninety-nine yards and didn't reach the end zone, lost an uncharacteristic fumble, and the Vols drove to a touchdown to cut the margin to two points. Tennessee then recovered an onside kick and maneuvered into field goal range in the game's final seconds. Daniel Lincoln lined up to attempt a forty-four yard field goal that would have won the game, but Alabama's mammoth defensive lineman, Terrence Cody, crashed through the middle and blocked the kick as time expired.

It was the second blocked kick of the game for Cody, a senior from Fort Myers, Florida, who was billed at 354 pounds but may have been closer to 400. His heroics saved a 12–10 victory. "Terrence Cody probably had three tackles that whole game, but he stepped up two plays in particular to block a field goal earlier in the game and blocked one at the end to give us the win," Anders says. "Guys always stepped up when their number was called."

To some on the Alabama sideline, it began to feel like fate. "I think things just fell into place," Arenas says. "It was our year. When you go through a season and things just fall into your hands, it's like you must be living right because good things are happening."

Alabama escaped with an 8–0 record, 5–0 in SEC play, and had an open date to get over its fatigue, bumps, and bruises. But another test was waiting as soon as Alabama returned to the field. LSU arrived at Bryant-Denny Stadium with a 7–1 record and number nine national ranking, and its own hopes of playing for the national championship.

An epic, hard-nosed battle ensued. LSU led 7–3 at the half and 15–10 going into the fourth quarter. Leigh Tiffin kicked the second of his three field goals, a twenty yarder, early in the final period, to cut the margin to two points. Alabama got a crucial stop on third and one when McClain and Cody stuffed Stevan Ridley on a third-and-one run.

On first and ten after the punt, Jones made the play of the game to give Alabama the lead. He caught a screen pass from McElroy and bolted seventy-three yards down the left sideline for a touchdown. Tiffin tacked on another field goal from forty yards out to give the Crimson Tide its winning margin of 24–15 and clinching the SEC Western Division title.

Ingram, coming off a 144-yard, twenty-two-carry performance

against LSU, ran through Mississippi State's defense for 149 yards and two scores on nineteen carries in a 31–3 victory, and added two more touchdowns and 102 yards on just eleven rushes in an abbreviated appearance in a 45–0 dominant performance over Chattanooga to take Alabama's record to 11–0.

However, the regular season wouldn't be over until Alabama had traveled to the Plains to take on its in-state rival, Auburn. The Tigers were 7–4 and had only won three conference games. They had nothing to lose and played like it with a series of trick plays early in the game. Receiver Terrell Zachery scored on a sixty-seven-yard reverse on Auburn's opening possession, and the Tigers put together a thirteen-play scoring drive after recovering an onside kick to make it 14–0.

Alabama regained its composure and battled back to tie it up by halftime. "They ran out of bullets," Arenas says. "All their firepower, nothing worked for them after that." Auburn kept Ingram in check, holding him to just thirty yards, and held Alabama to seventy-three total rushing yards on the day. Jones came up big, catching nine passes for ninety-three yards as McElroy passed for 218 yards and two scores, a big completion coming at the end of a game-winning drive that will live in crimson fame.

Alabama trailed when it took over midway through the fourth quarter. McElroy directed a fifteen-play, seventy-nine-yard drive that ate up more than seven minutes before it was capped by a four-yard touchdown toss to Upchurch with a minute and twenty-four seconds to go. The Tide's defense put the finishing touches on a 26–21 Iron Bowl victory. "I have never been more proud of my football team," Saban said after the game. "I said that it would be our most significant and our greatest accomplishment if we came down here and won this game." That victory kept Alabama in the thick of the national championship hunt, and players relished the chance to take on the Florida Gators again for the SEC title.

Florida had gained the number one spot in the rankings after

Alabama's close call against Tennessee, while the Crimson Tide
entered the league title game in the number two spot—a role rever-
sal from the previous year. That didn't matter to Alabama. Players
didn't just want to win the SEC; they wanted to do so against the
Gators. They hadn't forgotten. "There was no way they were going
to win that game after the feeling they put on us the season before,"
Arenas says. "That was our mind set. I think they even knew."

Florida was defending national champion coming into a game
where both teams were undefeated, but it wasn't even close. Alabama won 32–13, with McElroy, a junior from Southlake, Texas,
winning MVP honors after throwing for 239 yards and a touchdown on just twelve completions. Ingram gashed the Gators for
113 yards and three scores on twenty-six attempts and caught a
pair of passes for seventy-six yards. Florida quarterback Tim Tebow
looked dejected on the sideline as the final moments ran off the
clock. Alabama's stout defense held Florida to 335 yards while the
Tide rolled to 490. "We put a lot of pressure on Tebow. We knew
what plays they were going to run before they ran them. That's how
well prepared we were," Anders says.

Alabama won its twenty-second SEC championship and it's first
since 1999. Alabama earned a Bowl Championship Series national
title date with Texas in Pasadena, California, with the victory, but
first got to pause for an historic occasion.

The one jewel that had escaped the Crimson Tide through all
of its glory in college football history was finally captured when
Ingram became Alabama's first Heisman Trophy winner. Ingram
ran for 1,658 yards and seventeen touchdowns on 271 carries that
season while adding 334 receiving yards on fourteen receptions
with three more scores. Heisman voters recognized his contribution
to Alabama's undefeated run and he accepted the trophy in New
York City a week after the SEC title game. "I'm a little overwhelmed
right now," Ingram said as he broke into tears of joy after seeing
his mother, Shonda, crying in the audience when he looked down

from the podium to start his acceptance speech. After the ceremony, Ingram confessed that the magnitude of the event washed over him as he took the stage. "At first I was really calm, kind of relaxed," he said. "But then my heart started beating faster. I saw my mom crying, and I sort of broke down, too. When I was shaking hands with the other (past) winners, I was kind of in a daze. It was a crazy feeling."

Ingram was also named SEC Player of the Year on offense by the Associated Press. McClain won the Butkus Award as the nation's outstanding linebacker and league defensive player of the year honors. Arenas, an underrecruited talent from Tampa, Florida, who fell just short of setting the all-time career punt return record, was named the SEC's top special teams player. But there was a trophy left to capture: a crystal one. Alabama would still need to beat the Texas Longhorns to win the national title.

With the San Gabriel Mountains looming in the background, visible from the Rose Bowl Stadium where Alabama's national championship tradition began, the Crimson Tide prevailed. Alabama sent Texas's highly decorated quarterback, Colt McCoy (winner of the Maxwell Award and Walter Camp Foundation's player of the year award) to the sideline with a shoulder injury on the Longhorns' fifth snap of the game, when Marcell Dareus buried him on an option play.

Texas still managed to take an early 6–0 lead from a couple of field goals, but Alabama didn't blink. Ingram and Richardson both scored to make it 14–6. Tiffin kicked a field goal, and Dareus intercepted a shovel pass and returned it twenty-eight yards for a touchdown in the final seconds of the first half to put Alabama up 24–6.

Garret Gilbert, McCoy's backup, got in a rhythm in the third quarter, twice connecting with Jordan Shipley for touchdowns, but Alabama's defense took over to set up the scoring opportunities that allowed the Tide to put the game away. Arenas intercepted a pair of passes, and Anders forced a fumble by sacking Gilbert deep in Texas territory in the final minutes. "That's one of those plays that just goes down in Alabama history," Anders says. "It comes on the highlights (on the video screens) before the home games and stuff. I think that play is going to live on much longer than I will. It's great to be a part of a play that everybody's going to remember and tell their kids about."

Tyrone King added a final interception in the closing seconds, and Alabama was able to take a knee to run out the clock on a 37–21 championship victory. Ingram ran for 116 yards and two scores. Richardson added 109 and two more. Together with the defensive effort, it was emblematic of Saban's brand of team football. "It just helped me to realize how important it is to play united with a group of guys," Arenas says, "and it taught me how to play like that and to do my job within it. If everybody plays like that, we can have that type of success."

The Texas win returned Alabama to the national championship scene. It was the end of an undefeated season, but the beginning of a new era of Crimson Tide dominance.

# TABLE 13

## 2009

Coach Nick Saban

National Champions, SEC Champions

Won 14 Lost 0

| Alabama | Opponent | | Location | Date |
|---|---|---|---|---|
| 34 | Virginia Tech | 24 | Atlanta | Sept. 5 |
| 40 | Florida International | 14 | Tuscaloosa | Sept. 12 |
| 53 | North Texas | 7 | Tuscaloosa | Sept. 19 |
| 35 | Arkansas | 7 | Tuscaloosa | Sept. 26 |
| 38 | Kentucky | 20 | Lexington | Oct. 3 |
| 22 | Ole Miss | 3 | Oxford | Oct. 10 |
| 20 | South Carolina | 6 | Tuscaloosa | Oct. 17 |
| 12 | Tennessee | 10 | Tuscaloosa | Oct. 24 |
| 24 | LSU | 15 | Tuscaloosa | Nov. 7 |
| 31 | Mississippi State | 3 | Starkville | Nov. 14 |
| 45 | Chattanooga | 0 | Tuscaloosa | Nov. 21 |
| 26 | Auburn | 21 | Auburn | Nov. 27 |
| 32 | Florida | 13 | Atlanta (SEC) | Dec. 5 |
| 37 | Texas (Rose Bowl) | 21 | Pasadena | Jan. 7 |
| 449 | | 164 | | |

## CHAPTER FOURTEEN

# 2011

## MAYOR WALTER MADDOX

### APRIL 27, 2011

When it comes to football at The University of Alabama, winning championships is really important in Tuscaloosa. Prior to April 27, 2011, my first sentence would have been held as an absolute. Larger-than-life coaches have created expectations unrivaled in the world of sports, especially in college football. For most, these expectations would have been suffocating, but for Alabama, and the city they called home, winning championships had become the standard. Anything less was failure, and trying to pretend otherwise was foolish.

Life is unfair. Life is fragile. These two truths converged unmercifully at 5:13 P.M., on Wednesday, April 27, when a deadly EF-4 tornado with winds of 193 mph swept into the southwestern edge of the city, taking aim at the heart of Tuscaloosa. Twelve percent of the city was destroyed in a matter of minutes. Tuscaloosa's world changed forever, along with how we experienced Alabama Football and what we expected from it.

### A CONFIDENT HOPE EMERGES

As dawn approached on the morning of April 30, I was in the Rosedale Community meeting with our first responders. When the sun rose over the horizon, it illuminated the devastation that had en-

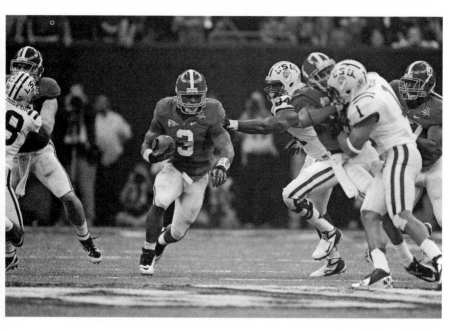

The offensive line opens a big running lane for Trent Richardson, photograph by Kent Gidley.

gulfed our city. In this rare, quiet moment, for the first time, the enormity of the devastation was overwhelming.

Over the past sixty hours, I had seen thriving neighborhoods removed from the map and talked to hundreds of people who were among the thousands who became homeless in an instant. I had met with business owners who had lost everything and countless individuals who had become unemployed in a matter of minutes, stood in deserted intersections where tens of thousands of cars once traveled, and saw our neighborhoods now being protected by the National Guard. I had met with family members who had lost loved ones or who were still searching the debris fields for signs of life. My actions felt as if I were throwing rocks against a battleship, yet I never doubted our resolve to fight and our ability to come back.

My story was one among thousands with a common theme

emerging out of the darkness—Hope. From Rosedale to Forest Lake, from Alberta to Holt, a confident hope was a familiar thread woven into our fabric, even with our backs squarely against the wall. With hope as our compass, we cleared debris, provided for the needy, and mourned for those lost. Tuscaloosa demonstrated to the world that hope was not something dreamed about in faraway places reserved only for fiction. Our hope was tangible and alive, connecting us in ways only our Maker could have imagined. Sustaining this confident hope—in an environment where fifty-three died, twelve hundred were injured, and thousands of homes, businesses, and churches were destroyed—was going to require all of us to meet the destruction of Mother Nature with the best of humanity.

## THE TIES THAT BIND

Within hours following the deadly tornado, head coach Nick Saban, Alabama players, coaches, and staff began volunteering in the areas of destruction. A new version of hope was taking the field, and it was of a championship caliber. Early on April 28, from a distance I saw Coach Saban on 15th Street distributing supplies, providing compassion, and instilling purpose. For most, even in Tuscaloosa, meeting the head football coach is rare. Whether it was a handshake, a pat on the back, or a simple conversation, Coach Saban was already setting the tone for Tuscaloosa's come back.

His presence in the early hours following the tornado signaled a powerful message that we were in this together. Reinforcing the team effort, Alabama's football team was investing sweat equity in the recovery zone, while creating plenty of smiles for fans who were meeting their favorite players in a very personal way. As with Coach Saban, interacting with the players was a rare treat and a welcomed distraction.

Although born out of tragic circumstances, a new relationship was being forged. For too long, we judged success by what the scoreboard displayed on Saturdays. Now, in the aftermath of one of Alabama's worst natural disasters, we realized something more personal and powerful; this team was now our team. We would mourn together. We would rebuild together. Win or lose, we would fight together.

> Hardship often prepares an ordinary person for
> an extraordinary destiny.
>
> —C.S. Lewis

In the 2011 season, one Alabama player captured the hearts of the nation: Carson Tinker. Although he was very good at his craft, Carson's deep-felt connection with the public had nothing to do with him being a walk-on long-snapper. To the contrary, his response to adversity and the courage of his convictions transformed this ordinary player into an extraordinary hero of the storm. Carson miraculously survived the tornado with serious, but not life-threatening injuries. However, his girlfriend Ashley Harrison, who was with him during the storm, did not survive.

Whether intentional or unintentional, Carson allowed the Alabama family to feel his pain, relate to his loss and experience his faith. It was authentic and inspiring. With energy and passion, Carson accepted every invitation to share his story and Ashley's story. His genuine response to adversity was not lost on the people who knew him best. When Alabama was bestowed the 2011 Disney's Wide World of Sports Spirit Award for its efforts in the response and recovery from the tornado, Carson was selected by his teammates to accept the honor. This kind and deserving gesture was only exceeded by Carson's amazing courage to chart a new destiny for his team, his community, and himself.

## THE SEASON

Late spring yielded to summer, and, as 1.5 million cubic yards of debris was being cleared, enough to fill Bryant-Denny Stadium five times, a quiet anticipation was gaining momentum. With the scars of destruction fresh and the grief still real, the annual rite of passage into football season felt decidedly different but absolutely necessary.

As expected, Alabama began the season in dominating fashion, and this momentum carried itself to November 5 where the "Game of the Century" awaited. Every game is important. Every game counts, but the 2011 season was ultimately defined by two titanic struggles with the Louisiana State University Tigers that mirrored the resiliency of Tuscaloosa.

With Bryant-Denny Stadium literally rocking, the top two teams in the nation needed more than sixty minutes to decide the victor. LSU was tough, determined, and gritty. Just five years removed from Hurricane Katrina, LSU understood the wrath of Mother Nature and how the passion of football can serve as a conduit toward healing. On this night, for a few hours, on one of football's most hallowed grounds, the focus was winning, and it felt really good to be "primetime" on Saturday night in Tuscaloosa.

The game was as good as advertised. For Alabama, the ending was not storybook, at least not yet. With LSU's place kicker Drew Alleman's kick through the uprights in overtime, LSU escaped Tuscaloosa with a hard fought victory. The loss was devastating, but not soul crushing because we uniquely understood there is more to life than a football game. From the shadows of April 27, we also knew hope could never be extinguished, especially with this coach and this team fighting not only for a championship, but also for our city.

In the weeks following the "Game of the Century," Alabama did what it does best, which is win, including a convincing victory over Auburn University at Jordan-Hare Stadium in the annual Iron Bowl. Just as important, those who leapt in front of Alabama in the rankings after November 5 found themselves forfeiting opportunities. Most notably, between November 18 and 19, Oklahoma State University, the University of Oklahoma, and the University of Oregon all were beaten, which propelled Alabama back into the quest for a National Championship. Hope was strengthened.

## THE REMATCH

Fate is powerful and unrelenting, and on January 9, 2012, in the New Orleans Mercedes-Benz Superdome, the two best teams in college football once again battled for supremacy. Fate often has a sense of irony, and this rematch was validation. New Orleans, which had been the epicenter for the destructive force of Hurricane Katrina, was now playing host to two teams from two states who felt the heavy burdens of winning.

Unlike the battle two months earlier, Alabama dominated the rematch. The advantages that were not seized in their previous match-up were exploited by an unmoveable defense and a ball-controlling offense. In addition, the kicking game, which had been an Achilles heel in November, became a strength with Jeremy Shelley nailing five field goals. Although the score was relatively close until late in the fourth quarter, there was little doubt throughout the game that Alabama was going to secure its thirteenth national championship.

## A DEEPER MEANING

In Lars Anderson's "The Storm and the Tide," he quotes Coach Saban as emphatically reminding his team before heading out of the Superdome's tunnel that, "We fight, we fight, we fight!" His passionate command encapsulated our resilient spirit of the last 256 days between the tornado and winning the national championship.

The 2011 season didn't erase the pain of losing a loved one, a home, or a business. Yet it meant everything to our city. Whether it was Tuscaloosa's response to the tornado or Alabama's determined journey to the pinnacle of college football, it was never about winning championships. It was about fighting through our grief. It was about fighting through our despair in the face of a massive humanitarian tragedy. It was about fighting for Tuscaloosa and reclaiming hope.

---

TABLE 14

**2011**

Coach Nick Saban

National Champions

Won 12 Lost 1

| Alabama | Opponent | | Location | Date |
|---|---|---|---|---|
| 48 | Kent State | 7 | Tuscaloosa | Sept. 3 |
| 27 | Penn State | 11 | University Park | Sept. 10 |
| 41 | North Texas | 0 | Tuscaloosa | Sept. 17 |
| 38 | Arkansas | 14 | Tuscaloosa | Sept. 24 |
| 38 | Florida | 10 | Gainesville | Oct. 1 |
| 34 | Vanderbilt | 0 | Tuscaloosa | Oct. 8 |
| 52 | Ole Miss | 7 | Oxford | Oct. 15 |
| 37 | Tennessee | 6 | Tuscaloosa | Oct. 22 |
| 6 | LSU | 9 | Tuscaloosa | Nov. 5 |
| 24 | Mississippi State | 7 | Starkville | Nov. 12 |
| 45 | Georgia Southern | 21 | Tuscaloosa | Nov. 19 |
| 42 | Auburn | 14 | Auburn | Nov. 26 |
| 21 | LSU (Sugar Bowl) | 0 | New Orleans | Jan. 9 |
| 453 | | 106 | | |

## CHAPTER FIFTEEN

# 2012

## Tommy Deas and Barrett Jones

**C**hampionship seasons have defining moments. The defining moment for Alabama in the 2012 national title season occurred when the Crimson Tide was up by four touchdowns with seven minutes to go in Sun Life Stadium in Miami Gardens, Florida, in the final game of the season. It wasn't about Alabama's opponent, Notre Dame, nor was it even a crucial point in the game—they could have handed Alabama the crystal Bowl Championship Series trophy at halftime. It was about perfection, and a passion for winning football.

Alabama lined up on second and six at its own twenty-nine-yard line, looking to run clock. Notre Dame's defense shifted as the play clock ticked down, and center Barrett Jones pointed and changed the blocking call for the offensive line. A. J. McCarron saw that Alabama wasn't going to get the snap off in time and called timeout. Then he got in Jones's face and barked some expletives. Jones, in turn, shoved his quarterback with both hands. It was a strange sight with Alabama on the verge of its third national championship in four years, and second in a row. But it said everything about that team. "In a way it kind of represented the kind of commitment we did have to doing things the right way and the process and not worrying about the scoreboard and just playing the best game we could play," Jones says. "Definitely it was a manifestation of those desires in that moment. We ran out of time and (could have taken) a delay

Eddie Lacey breaks into the Notre Dame secondary, photograph by Jeri Gulsby.

of game, and that's unacceptable in our way of doing things. We never want to have any penalties and to shoot ourselves in the foot that way—he had some spirited words for me, and I kind of shoved him in reaction. It happened so quick I didn't really think about it."

Alabama won that game 42–14, and in doing so accomplished what it had set out to do. The 2012 season, you see, was about something greater than just winning a championship, and this team had known it since before the first snap. "A lot of the guys, I remember them saying we want to do something legendary," says Jones, who won the Rimington Trophy as the nation's outstanding center after being awarded the Outland Trophy as the country's top lineman the season before. "People, after a while, kind of forget who wins one championship here and there, but people would probably remember us for a while if we won two in a row, and especially if we won three out of four like that. We wanted to kind of create a dynasty."

A couple of days after Alabama returned from defeating LSU in the Superdome in New Orleans to claim the 2011 national championship, head coach Nick Saban called a team meeting for returning players. He congratulated them and informed them that there would be a parade. He had one more message: "I'm ready to move on to next year."

Jones had been on the 2009 national championship team and remembered how Alabama had fallen short the following season. No team had won back-to-back titles since Southern Cal in 2003 and 2004 (sharing one of those with Saban's LSU team in a split title year), and it hadn't been done outright since Nebraska in 1994 and 1995.

Now a fifth-year senior, the lineman from Germantown, Tennessee, saw a team with a different attitude coming off the 2011 championship. "In 2009, we definitely savored the victory more," he says. "You know, it was the first national championship that we'd won in a while, and a lot more of the leaders were leaving, and we were reloading a little bit. It was a different approach in 2012. We really wanted to win back to back. We knew it was something that hadn't been done in a long time and something that's very difficult." So the 2011 title celebration ended, really, before the parade. Players began offseason workouts with a mind to do something that would be historic.

Going into spring practice, the offensive line had potential to be the Crimson Tide's strength. Monstrous six feet six inches, 335-pound D. J. Fluker was entrenched at right tackle, and both Chance Warmack and Anthony Steen were returning at the guard positions. A six feet six inches, 310-pound sophomore Cyrus Kouandjio was emerging as a candidate at tackle.

The question was what to do with Jones, who was destined to go down as one of the most decorated players in the program's history. In 2011, he had won the Outland Trophy, the Jacobs Blocking Award as the best blocker in the Southeastern Conference and the Wuerffel Trophy for community service and athletic and academic achievement. By the time 2012's hardware was in, he had added the Rimington Trophy, the William V. Campbell Trophy (known as the "Academic Heisman"), and Academic All-America of the Year honors. And that doesn't count his first-team All-American and All-SEC awards.

He just needed a place to play. By the end of his career, Jones played all five positions on the line, and Alabama needed someone in the middle to run the show his senior year. "That was a big topic," Jones recalls. "I had played left tackle the year before, but I went to playing center in the spring because in our system, we usually like to have an experienced guy there. It's just kind of a core belief of what we do, having that guy that's steady, that has experience, I guess intelligent, that makes the decisions and calls. I'm not saying that to brag on myself, that's just our philosophy. They made that move, and we were trying to figure out who the five would be. We finally got that lineup set, and once we got to playing, and in a rhythm, I realized it could be a really special unit."

There was another cog in that offensive line machine, tight end Michael Williams, who blocked with brute force even though he didn't catch a lot of passes. "He was definitely our sixth man on the offensive line," Jones says. "When he was on the field, our yards per carry probably went way up versus when he was not."

That unit fueled an offense that evolved not only to be powerful but also explosive. Alabama went on to average 38.7 points per game, rushing for 3,185 yards and passing for 3,052 yards with thirty-seven touchdowns from the ground game and another thirty-one through the air.

Eddie Lacey and T. J. Yeldon powered the running game, and

Kevin Norwood was a dependable target at wideout while a young star named Amari Cooper emerged as a nearly unstoppable deep threat. What made it work was the balance provided by the arm of McCarron, a junior from Mobile who had begun to come into his own in the national title win over LSU the year before when the game plan put the ball in his hands. Alabama became a team that could win by run or by pass. "We all saw what kind of talent he had and what kind of leadership abilities," Jones says. "That first year he started, to a certain degree he didn't have to win every game for us. We had a lot of games where we could have easily won with him being that 'game manager.' Coming into the 2012 season, we knew he could really become that dynamic passer. He didn't turn the ball over and still made those smart decisions—still managed the game in a good way—but became a very, very successful starter."

The Crimson Tide had already come to set the gold standard for defense under Saban, and this unit—with leaders like linebacker C. J. Mosley, cornerback Dee Milliner, and lineman Jesse Williams, an Australian wildman who had a personality as big as his game— lived up to that billing, shutting out four opponents and holding another seven to two touchdowns or less. Alabama allowed an average of less than eleven points per game.

Alabama swaggered into the season with a number two pre-season ranking by the Associated Press, behind only Southern Cal, which crashed and burned to a 7–6 record under young coach Lane Kiffin, who later joined Alabama's national championship history as an offensive coordinator. The Crimson Tide opened with a 41–14 bullying of eighth-ranked Michigan in Cowboys Stadium in Arlington, Virginia. The opponent and the venue got Alabama's attention. "I always loved playing a name-brand opponent to start the season," Jones says. "Michigan was a great example of that, a very historic team with a lot of great players."

Saban, a creature of habit, broke routine to take the team to the stadium before the game so players could get used to playing beneath the world's largest big-screen video board, which is suspended over the field. "Coach Saban normally gives a Gene Hackman-like 'Hoosiers' speech about the field being one-hundred-yards long and fifty-three-yards wide, so we shouldn't have to have a walk-through," Jones says, "but he made an exception for that."

There were plenty of highlights on the big screen that night. McCarron passed for 199 yards and two touchdowns. Yeldon ran for 111 yards and a score, and Mosley returned an interception for another. "I kind of suspected that we were going to have a really good team, but I remember coming away from that game thinking that we could have probably one of the best offenses Alabama had ever seen," Jones says.

The Tide marched through its next three opponents by a 127-7 margin, beating Western Kentucky (35–0), Arkansas on the road (52-0), and Florida Atlantic (40–7), moving up to the top spot in the polls along the way. Alabama hardly slowed down in the following weeks, defeating Ole Miss at home (33–14) and then going on the road to down Missouri (42–10) and Tennessee (44–13). After a 38–7 win at Bryant-Denny Stadium over eleventh-ranked Mississippi State, Alabama was 8–0 and hadn't been tested going into its bye week. "We were kind of rolling through the middle of the season there," Jones says. "When we played our best, we were going to be really hard to beat."

Coming out of its break, however, Alabama didn't play its best. That might have had something to do with the aura of a stadium in Baton Rouge, Louisianna, known as Death Valley, and a fifth-ranked LSU team with a 7–1 record. The Tigers outplayed Alabama for more than fifty-eight minutes, but were holding onto a slim 17–14 lead. Alabama got the ball back one last time at its own twenty-eight yard line with a minute and thirty-four seconds to go.

The Crimson Tide was ready for the challenge. "Everybody knew something special was about to happen," Jones says. "We addressed that in the huddle during a timeout before that drive." McCarron and Norwood had uncommon chemistry, and it showed on that possession. The first three plays were completions of eighteen, fifteen, and eleven yards, with Norwood getting out of bounds on the last two catches. "Kevin was such an unsung hero for us his whole career in a way," Jones says. "He always made huge plays in big moments."

After an incompletion, McCarron tossed a screen pass to Yeldon, who galloped twenty-eight yards into the end zone for the winning score as Alabama prevailed 21–17. "I told our guys that we were going to have to keep fighting in this game and keep punching until we knock them out," Saban said in his postgame news conference.

Alabama, however, didn't see the counterpunch that was coming a week later, Texas A&M, led by a hotshot gunslinger named Johnny Manziel, who was a redshirt freshman on his way to claiming the Heisman Trophy. He had a radar-like awareness in the pocket, a rocket arm, and uncanny quickness. Undaunted by Alabama's ranking and its record, the fifteenth-ranked Aggies pulled a stunning upset (29–24) on Alabama's home field in Tuscaloosa.

Manziel led A&M to three touchdowns and a 20–0 lead in the first quarter. Before it was over, he amassed 345 yards, 253 through the air. Alabama tried to claw its way back in the game, with Lacy rushing for ninety-two yards and a touchdown and Cooper, the freshman wideout sensation, hauling in six receptions for 136 yards and a score. McCarron passed for 309 yards to try to keep pace with Manziel, but an interception at the goal line and a fumble in A&M territory cost Alabama a chance to come from behind again.

The loss still lingers. "We really wanted to be undefeated," Jones says. "There's just something about being undefeated, and we felt we were good enough to accomplish that. I think it still eats at a lot of guys today."

No one had to tell Alabama players that the defeat was a serious setback. But they were mindful that a year earlier Alabama had lost to LSU and still earned a spot in the championship game to win it all. "Spirits were very low for a moment after the game," Jones says, "but Coach Saban stood up and just kind of refocused us. We knew what could happen; we had been there the year before and seen what could happen in that scenario. Guys bought into that."

The Crimson Tide dropped to fourth in the rankings, behind undefeated Kansas State, Oregon and Notre Dame. Two of those, most likely, would have to lose late in the season for Alabama to have a chance. The Crimson Tide no longer had any margin for error.

It didn't take long for the Alabama to get the help it needed. A week after what seemed a devastating defeat, Alabama steamrolled Western Carolina (49–0) and sat back while Baylor upended Kansas State and Stanford knocked Oregon out of the title hunt. That left Alabama, suddenly back in the thick of the title picture at number two behind still-undefeated Notre Dame, to close out the regular season against rival Auburn, which was reeling. The Tigers were 3–8, winless in the conference, and head coach Gene Chizik was on his way out.

Alabama showed no mercy, winning 49–0 as McCarron— who had broken the school record for touchdown passes a week earlier—threw for four scores and Lacy ran for 131 yards and two more touchdowns. "It was over quick," Jones says. "I was very surprised the way Auburn showed up for the game. I think there was a lot of turmoil going on. On their side there were just a lot of guys yelling at each other on the field, a lot of unhappiness all around."

Alabama, on the other hand, had reason to celebrate. The victory clinched the SEC Western Division title and set up a *de facto* national semifinal against third-ranked, once-defeated Georgia in the league title game. The SEC champion, it was presumed, would face 12-0 Notre Dame for college football's championship.

The Crimson Tide and Georgia went toe to toe in Atlanta, swapping the lead as they traded heavyweight haymakers. The Bulldogs went ahead 21–10 with six minutes and thirty-one seconds to go in the third quarter on a blocked punt return, and Alabama was on the ropes. Alabama turned to its running game and drove seventy-seven yards in four plays, helped by a pass interference penalty, with Yeldon carrying for four, thirty-one, two, and finally ten yards for a touchdown. Alabama forced a Georgia punt, and Lacy ran through a tiring Bulldog defense for thirty-two, fifteen, and fourteen yards. Yeldon spelled him for a thirteen-yard gain, and Lacy returned to crash into the end zone for a one-yard touchdown, and Alabama was ahead 25–21 early in the fourth quarter.

But the drama was far from over. Georgia answered with a ten-yard touchdown run by Todd Gurley on its ensuing possession, and Alabama stalled at the fifty yardline when it got the ball back. The Crimson Tide got a defensive stop and went back to the run, pounding away to set up a play-action pass to Cooper, who hauled in McCarron's throw for a forty-five yard score and a 32–28 lead with a little over three minutes to go.

The Bulldogs were not done. They got the ball back with a minute and eight seconds left and eighty-five yards to go. Quarterback Aaron Murray passed with precision to get Georgia to the Alabama eight-yard line. Taking the snap as the clock ran under ten seconds, Murray looked for a target and released the ball as a blitzing Mosley crashed through to deflect it. Flanker Chris Conley caught it at the five but went down inbounds and the clock ran out.

Confetti rained from the Georgia Dome roof as Alabama basked in its SEC championship victory. Lacy ran for 181 yards and two touchdowns on twenty carries, and was named the game's Most Valuable Player, with Yeldon adding 153 yards on twenty-five attempts and Cooper hauling in seven catches for 127 yards, including the big touchdown.

Jones sustained a foot injury in the second quarter. He had trainers tape it up and returned to finish, but would later find out that he had torn ligaments in what turned out to be a serious injury. "It was excruciating," he later confessed. "It was very painful. It was tough, but there was no way I was not going to finish that football game." Nor was he going to miss out on the national title game, a storied matchup against Notre Dame. His foot was placed in a protective boot, and he stayed off of it for three weeks or more, never practicing. Instead he watched film, and liked what he saw. "I thought it would be a tough test when they announced it," he says, "but when we started watching film and trying to figure out who these guys were, we all had a pretty good feeling that we had a chance to win it convincingly."

The film did not lie. Alabama pushed around a smaller, overmatched Notre Dame team from the start on the way to a 28–0 halftime lead and was up 35–0 before the Fighting Irish finally scored in the third quarter, but the Crimson Tide wasn't going to allow a dramatic comeback, and rolled to victory. McCarron passed for 264 yards and four touchdowns, with Cooper grabbing six receptions for 105 yards and two scores. Lacy ran loose for 140 yards and a score and Yeldon added 108 rushing yards and another touchdown. Alabama's defense allowed just thirty-two rushing yards and safety HaHa Clinton-Dix picked off a pass.

The victory was the forty-ninth for Alabama's senior class, which left with three national championship rings and two SEC titles. "We've had a lot of great players who have worked very hard," Saban said in the aftermath. "Because we've had a great team, we've had a significant amount of success." Saban had told his squad that he didn't believe winning a second championship in a row would be any tougher than winning the one before it. Perhaps it was a bit of psychology, or maybe that was his viewpoint.

Jones, who had that brief squabble with his quarterback on the field in the crowning game, also begs to differ with his coach. "We accomplished this goal that is so hard to accomplish," Jones says. "Winning back to back, I think, is harder. Coach Saban says it's not, but it is."

# TABLE 15

**2012**

Coach Nick Saban

National Champions, SEC Champions

Won 13 Lost 1

| Alabama | Opponent | | Location | Date |
|---|---|---|---|---|
| 41 | Michigan | 14 | Arlington | Sept. 1 |
| 35 | Western Kentucky | 0 | Tuscaloosa | Sept. 8 |
| 52 | Arkansas | 0 | Fayetteville | Sept. 15 |
| 40 | Florida Atlantic | 7 | Tuscaloosa | Sept. 22 |
| 33 | Ole Miss | 14 | Tuscaloosa | Sept. 29 |
| 42 | Missouri | 10 | Columbia | Oct. 13 |
| 44 | Tennessee | 13 | Knoxville | Oct. 20 |
| 38 | Mississippi State | 7 | Tuscaloosa | Oct. 27 |
| 21 | LSU | 17 | Baton Rouge | Nov. 3 |
| 24 | Texas A&M | 29 | Tuscaloosa | Nov. 10 |
| 49 | Western Carolina | 0 | Tuscaloosa | Nov. 17 |
| 49 | Auburn | 0 | Tuscaloosa | Nov. 24 |
| 32 | Georgia | 28 | Atlanta | Dec. 1 |
| 42 | Notre Dame (Orange Bowl) | 14 | Miami Gardens | Jan. 7 |
| 542 | | 153 | | |

## CHAPTER SIXTEEN

# 2015

## PHIL SAVAGE

In 2009 when I joined the Crimson Tide Sports Network as the football color analyst, there was no way to know that Alabama was about to embark on one of the most historical runs in the annals of the college game. Broadcasting alongside Eli Gold would have been exciting enough, but to see Nick Saban, a coach I worked directly with at the Cleveland Browns from 1991–93, implement The Process and witness the success Alabama has enjoyed over the past seven years has been a very rewarding experience and one that I will cherish forever. With that said, I am truly honored to chronicle the journey of the 2015 team that opened the season in Arlington, Texas, with probably more questions than answers, and ended it in the Valley of the Sun as national champions for the sixteenth time in school history.

Despite the annual high expectations and a top-five preseason ranking, there were two major issues for the Crimson Tide to address as they opened training camp in August: who would be the starting quarterback and can the defensive secondary improve on a disappointing showing in 2014? For the second year in a row, Coach Saban conducted an open competition for the quaterback job, and the pass defense had finished fifty-eighth the year before in the final NCAA statistics.

Mobile native and Florida State transfer Jake Coker, sophomore Cooper Bateman, and junior Alec Morris emerged as the three pri-

Tight end O. J. Howard breaks free for a touchdown. Photo by Robert Sutton.

mary contenders for the quarterback spot, but none of them distinguished themselves in the first two noteworthy scrimmages. Saban opted to keep the contest shrouded in secrecy, but ultimately, opted for the senior Coker to open the Wisconsin game at AT&T Stadium.

The Badgers presented a challenge because of their ability to run the football and recent history of success on defense. However, two themes emerged at the home of the Dallas Cowboys for this Alabama team: a dominant tailback named Derrick Henry and a formidable front seven that essentially went two-deep at every defensive line and linebacker position. Henry broke loose on fourth and one and sprinted away from the Wisconsin defense for a thirty-seven yard score that would be the first of his school-record twenty-eight touchdowns in 2015. Linebacker Reggie Ragland led the Tide with twelve tackles and set the tempo for a unit that would establish itself as the best in the nation against the run. Final score: Alabama 35, Wisconsin 17. After a 37–10 home opening win vs. Middle Tennessee, the Crimson Tide would turn its attention to their Southeastern Conference opener against Ole Miss.

In 2014, I attended the Arizona at Oregon game on a Thursday night in connection with my Reese's Senior Bowl duties before flying to Memphis in advance of our game against Ole Miss. On the route from Atlanta to Memphis that Friday, my plane's engine was "back-firing" as we took off and the entire jet was lurching forward in the air. After circling back to make an emergency landing, we ended up being nearly four hours late, but thankful to be alive! Nevertheless, that event was only a precursor of what was to come the next day. Bama was upset by Ole Miss when Kenyan Drake suffered a season-ending dislocated ankle and center Ryan Kelly went down midway in the third quarter with a sprained knee. The Tide missed a third quarter field goal and then gave up two late scores before coming up short on a desperation two-minute drive that ended with an interception in the Rebels' end zone.

All of this is to say, there was no way Bama could have another "Murphy's Law" type outing against the Rebels, especially in Tuscaloosa, where they had won just a single game in the history of the series. But, it happened again. Alabama fumbled the opening kickoff, proceeded to turn the football over six total times, and at one point fell behind 43–24 with ten minutes and two seconds left in the game. After giving Cooper Bateman his first start, Saban and company opted for Coker, and he rallied the Tide back to a score at 43–37. However, every time Alabama got within one play of changing the game something bad happened, including a tipped sixty-six yard touchdown reception and another seventy-three yarder on the dreaded "pop pass" when the Tide vacated coverage on the Rebels' wide receiver. Give Ole Miss credit though, they did what they had to do to win in Bryant-Denny Stadium, but for Alabama, there was a silver lining to the loss. One, the team never gave up, and two, Jake Coker emerged as a leader and as the obvious choice at quarterback for this 2015 squad. Final score: Ole Miss 43, Alabama 37.

With their backs against the wall and in playoff mode by the end of September, Louisiana-Monroe was disposed of 34–0, and now all of the attention turned to Georgia. Alabama's trip to Athens had been circled by the national media and fans of both teams as one of the most pivotal games of the entire college season. Many pundits claimed the Bama dynasty was over and that the Bulldogs would get their revenge for having lost the SEC championship game in 2012 when they fell five yards short of the goal line with time expiring. However, Mother Nature did the Tide a favor with torrential rains associated with Hurricane Joaquin. Because of the weather conditions, offensive coordinator Lane Kiffin played to the strengths of his offense with the downhill running of Henry, the play-action passing of Coker, and the big play talent of wide receiver Calvin Ridley. Eddie Jackson had a fifty-yard pick-six, and the Tide humiliated Georgia Between the Hedges. Final score: Alabama 38, Georgia 10.

When Bret Bielema became the Arkansas coach, he brought his Big Ten style with him from Wisconsin, which revolved around a huge offensive line and a powerful running game. In a little more than two seasons, he led the Razorbacks from the embarrassing aftermath of the Bobby Petrino era to a bowl win over Texas in 2014 and elevated expectations for his third squad in 2015. By the time the Hogs arrived in Tuscaloosa, they had misfired against Toledo in a loss at home and also gift-wrapped the Texas A&M contest to the Aggies. They were a team that could easily be overlooked, which made them a dangerous opponent, especially considering they had lost to Alabama on a blocked extra point the year before in Fayetteville. But, as much as Bielema wanted to line up and play jaw-to-jaw with Bama, he simply did not have the defense to get that done yet, and the Tide's front seven proved again that they would be almost impossible to run against between the tackles. All-SEC tailback Alex Collins was limited to twenty-six yards on twelve carries, while Derrick Henry pounded out ninety-five yards on twenty-seven attempts and scored another touchdown for the Tide's fifth victory of the year. Final score: Alabama 27, Arkansas 14.

Since Coach Saban's arrival in 2007, no program in America had gotten more out of true freshmen than the Crimson Tide. After Alabama shellacked Texas A&M and their version of the Air Raid offense 59–0 in 2014, the Crimson Tide secondary seemed to regress and gave up 456 yards in the air to Auburn and then another 256 in the playoff loss to Ohio State.

The first time I saw Minkah Fitzpatrick was on a YouTube video that showed him doing defensive-back footwork drills in the snow on top of an apartment building in New Jersey. The next time I saw him was on the field during preseason camp, and it was obvious that the Tide had recruited the right prospect once again. Dripping with talent, he had the height, arm length, foot quickness, change-of-direction ability, and ball skills needed to play as a true freshman. It would be just a matter of time before he mastered his role and would hit the field.

With A&M almost exclusively using a four-wide receiver set, the Alabama defense employed the use of their six-defensive back or Dime package with Minkah aligned over the Aggies' own sensational freshman, and maybe the fastest player in the country, Christian Kirk. Not only did the Tide once again contain the A&M passing game, they put together a school-record of three pick-sixes, including two by Fitzpatrick and another one by Eddie Jackson. The defensive effort was so spectacular, especially after the shut-down of Arkansas's vaunted run game the week before, that everyone now knew this defense was complete with the final piece of the puzzle being a young freshman who had perfected his craft atop a snow-covered East Coast skyscraper. Final Score: Alabama 41, Texas A&M 23.

The passing game began the 2016 season with essentially a blank page at quarterback and receiver. With Ardarius Stewart being the leading pass catcher with twelve grabs in 2015 as a rotational backup, the Alabama aerial attack was going to be a work in progress to be sure. Once Saban arrived in 2007, the Tide had dominated the "Third Saturday in October," but hardcore Alabama fans understood this rivalry probably better than the players themselves. Through three quarters and seven minutes, coach Butch Jones's squad relied on their two-headed offense led by quaterback Joshua Dobbs and running back Jalen Hurd in forging to a 14–13 lead with a little over five minutes and forty-nine seconds remaining in the contest. With the season on the line, Coker and company responded with an eight-play, seventy-one yard touchdown drive that included key pass completions to both super freshman Calvin Ridley and Ardarius Stewart. The passing game had evolved, and Alabama had emerged with yet another way to win a game. Final Score: Alabama 19, Tennessee 14.

After the traditional bye week before the LSU game, both the Tide and Tigers arrived in Tuscaloosa with the idea that the most physical team inside Bryant-Denny Stadium would win the game. LSU boasted the leading Heisman Trophy contender in running back Leonard Fournette who was averaging 193.1 yards per game on the season. The Tigers lined up and actually tried to overpower the Alabama front seven, and after one series of downs, it was obvious their offensive game plan was doomed. Fournette finished with nineteen carries for thirty-one yards, and the Crimson Tide got more good news when Arkansas upset Ole Miss 53–52 in overtime. And by the way, all Derrick Henry did was rush for 210 yards on thirty-eight carries with another three touchdowns and literally snatch the Heisman right out of Fournette's hands. Final score: Alabama 30, LSU 16.

The always-concerning "letdown" game vs. Mississippi State did not happen in 2015 because, again, the defensive front dominated the action along the line of scrimmage. From the opening snap, All-SEC quarterback Dak Prescott was harassed and hounded by a unit that racked up nine sacks on the afternoon. On the downside, Alabama running back Kenyan Drake suffered a fractured arm while covering a kickoff, which put even more of a burden on Henry to carry the load through the rest of the regular season and into Atlanta. Final score: Alabama 31, Mississippi State 6.

In the final home appearance by the Crimson Tide, Charleston Southern was dispatched 56–6 behind another touchdown punt return by senior Cyrus Jones, and it was on to the Iron Bowl. Going back to 1989, the trip to Auburn is always an unsettling, teeth-clenching journey, and this game was no different, especially with so much hype surrounding the despicable Kick-Six ending in 2013. However, this Auburn team was no match for Alabama. Nursing a nine-point lead in the fourth quarter, Lane Kiffin called for fourteen straight runs for Henry, and Henry would secure the Heisman Trophy with a record-breaking forty-six carries and 271-yard night on the Plains. And, not to be outdone, place kicker Adam Griffith returned to Jordan-Hare and made five field goals to help extinguish his own nightmare from two years earlier. Final score: Alabama 29, Auburn 13.

David Norrie is a good friend of mine and the color analyst for ESPN's national radio broadcasts. Before the Sugar Bowl vs. Oklahoma at the end of the 2013 campaign, he asked me for an evaluation on Derrick Henry who had not played much during the regular season. I gave him a one-word answer, "Secretariat"! Whether you know him as number 2, "El Tractorcito," or the 2015 Heisman Trophy winner, Henry is a humble giant of a running back who put this Alabama team on his broad shoulders and strong legs and carried the football a phenomenal 395 times in fifteen total games. While doing this, he remained the hardest worker on the team and represented the program in a first class manner during every interview and awards show throughout his career.

Florida, under the direction of former Alabama assistant coach Jim McElwain, surprised everyone with a fast start to the 2015 season and with wins over Tennessee, Missouri, and Georgia, earning their place in the SEC Championship game by early November. The problem for the Gators was that the quaterback that helped them get there was suspended in mid-October, and their offense had really sputtered down the stretch. The only way Florida could win in Atlanta would be with their defense creating turnovers and notching a touchdown themselves in conjunction with a special teams score, too. The Florida defense was fast and aggressive and equipped with NFL talent at all three levels of play (defensive line, linebackers, and secondary). Geared to stop Henry, Florida tried to put the game on Coker's shoulders and depend on their defensive backs to hold up in one-on-one coverage. Through the first quarter and a-half, the Gators stymied the Tide because of their overall defensive speed and physicality. However, once again Coker made two big plays down the field when he put the ball up for Ridley who elevated between two Florida defenders and came down with possession at the three yard line to set up another Henry touchdown plunge. And then, after avoiding the rush and stepping up inside the edge, Coker heaved one into the end zone, and Ardarius Stewart climbed the ladder for a thirty-two yard touchdown between two grasping-for-air Gators. Final score: Alabama 29, Florida 15.

With a twenty-fifth SEC title in hand, Alabama earned a spot in the College Football Playoff for a second consecutive year. In looking at Michigan State, their upcoming semifinal opponent, the Spartans' preference was to stay in a base 4–3 defense against virtually every offensive personnel grouping, except in obvious third and long situations. The invitation was there for Alabama to deploy their three-wide receiver or "Blue" package and create mismatches with Calvin Ridley and Richard Mullaney in the slot against the Michigan State linebackers and/or safeties. With MSU geared to stop Henry, offensive coordinator Lane Kiffin knew this would be a night of tough sledding for Henry, but could be a special evening for his passing game. And what a CFP semifinal it proved to be for quarterback Jake Coker.

I can't recall an Alabama player being criticized and questioned more than Coker upon his arrival as a graduate transfer from Florida State in the spring of 2014. Blake Sims beat him out for the starting quarterback job that year; so many people assumed that he just did not have it. That theme developed further in the spring of 2015 and during the preseason practices too. What many did not realize was that although Coker stands six feet five inches, has a huge arm, and deceiving mobility. His most important traits were toughness and a fear of failure. Virtually every game he made a winning play that did not show up in the statistics, like throwing a pass away or scrambling for no gain to preserve field position. Maybe his signature snap was when he absolutely blasted a Texas A&M linebacker in finishing a run in College Station, but the game he'll be best remembered for was this outing vs. Michigan State when he went twenty-five of thirty for 268 yards and two touchdowns.

Dabo Swinney, the Clemson head coach, dreamed of playing for the Crimson Tide as a boy and did that from 1989–92. He then coached for Gene Stallings and learned the ways of Alabama Football. He is an excellent recruiter and when I studied the Tigers on video, I projected at least thirteen to fifteen of their starters as players that could do the same or contribute in a major way for this Alabama team (as a comparison in 2012, Notre Dame had seven or eight players that could play for Alabama). The Tide indeed faced their toughest challenge in a national title game under Nick Saban. While MSU invited Alabama's offense to attack the perimeter, it appeared that Clemson would be the exact opposite. They were ter-rifically talented on the edges with cornerbacks MacKensie Alex-ander and Cordrea Tankersley. That meant the middle of the field would be the best option for the Tide, and Derrick Henry broke free on a fifty yard run right between the hashmarks for a 7–0 lead. While the Alabama defense had made many adjustments over-the past nine seasons from a plodding 3–4 front built on size and strength to a unit with length and speed at literally all of the po-sitions, Clemson quaterback Deshaun Watson was one tough as-signment. He threw strike after strike, ran for the sticks, and gen-erally had every Alabama fan in the nation shaking their heads in amazement at what he seemed to singlehandedly be doing against the formidable Tide defense. By the time Alabama got to the fourth quarter of this back-and-forth affair, and with the score tied 24–24, Saban had seen enough and called for a surprise onside kick. If The Process is what his legacy will be, then this will be the signature play of his sterling coaching career. Executed with brilliant pre-cision, kicker Adam Griffith punched an absolutely perfect end-under-end "pass" to Marlon Humphrey just beyond the widest Clemson player on their kickoff return team. It was THE moment that changed the momentum in favor of the Crimson Tide. O. J. Howard had the night of his career with five catches for 208 yards and two touchdowns and combined with D. J. Pettway's blocked field goal at the end of the first half and Kenyan Drake's ninety-five yard kickoff return in the fourth quarter, Alabama won their fourth national championship in seven seasons by proving to be a complete team in every phase of the game. Final score: Alabama 45, Clemson 40.

# TABLE 16

## 2015

### Coach Nick Saban

### National Champions, SEC Champions

### Won 14 Lost 1

| Alabama | Opponent | | Location | Date |
|---|---|---|---|---|
| 35 | Wisconsin | 17 | Arlington | Sept. 5 |
| 37 | Middle Tennessee State | 10 | Tuscaloosa | Sept. 12 |
| 37 | Ole Miss | 43 | Tuscaloosa | Sept. 19 |
| 34 | Louisiana-Monroe | 0 | Tuscaloosa | Sept. 26 |
| 38 | Georgia | 10 | Athens | Oct. 3 |
| 27 | Arkansas | 14 | Tuscaloosa | Oct. 10 |
| 41 | Texas A&M | 23 | College Station | Oct. 17 |
| 19 | Tennessee | 14 | Tuscaloosa | Oct. 24 |
| 30 | LSU | 16 | Tuscaloosa | Nov. 7 |
| 31 | Mississippi State | 6 | Starkville | Nov. 14 |
| 56 | Charleston Southern | 6 | Tuscaloosa | Nov. 21 |
| 29 | Auburn | 13 | Auburn | Nov. 28 |
| 29 | Florida | 15 | Atlanta | Dec. 5 |
| 38 | Michigan State (Cotton Bowl) | 0 | Arlington | Dec. 31 |
| 45 | Clemson (Fiesta Bowl) | 40 | Glendale | Jan. 11 |
| 526 | | 227 | | |

## CHAPTER SEVENTEEN

# The Other Five

## ALLEN BARRA

The Bowl Championship Series— or BCS—for determining the national college football champion is relatively new, and in the eyes of some purists not an improvement over the old system, where the Associated Press, the United Press International, the MacArthur Bowl committee, and just about any other group that could afford to put a letterhead on stationery simply ranked teams in the order they thought they should be ranked.

To many fans, one of the joys of college football was arguing the relative merits of the Woulda-Coulda-Shoulda contenders in the off-season. Let's call them the WCS. And no school has ever had more WCS champions than Alabama. Here are the stories of five of the best.

Alabama's first entry in the WCS was in 1945, and many grizzled Tide veterans think it ranks just behind the 1966 team as Alabama's strongest entry in that mythical series.

To begin with, it was yet another Alabama-underdog-wins-the-Rose-Bowl team. After the 1926, 1931, and 1935 Rose Bowls, you might have thought the West Coast sports press would have learned something, but, as one *Los Angeles Times* columnist wrote before the big game, "You've won in the Rose Bowl before, but, Alabama, you haven't played Southern Cal yet." Yes, and the Trojans had not yet played Alabama.

In truth, the Trojans didn't play much of anyone that year—they had to play UCLA twice to fill out their schedule and one of their opponents was tiny St. Mary's near San Francisco, who stuffed the Trojans 26–0. All in all, USC put up an okay 7–3 record but outscored their opponents by only 75 points. The Tide, spearheaded by their sensational halfback, Harry Gilmer, was a terror, winning all ten of their games by a margin of 396–66. Gilmer was listed as a running back, but like many tailbacks of his time he was also his team's most effective passer, famed for his "leaping passes" in which he would launch himself two and even three feet into the air to loft the ball over the heads of onrushing tacklers. It was, he once said, a style he developed while playing sand lot ball "out of desperation. It was the only way I could see to throw downfield." There's a sensational photo of him midair, jumping to send a pass downfield in the Tide's 25–7 victory over Tennessee at Legion Field in Birmingham. If you think white men can't jump, you should seek out the picture.

True, some of Alabama's opponents during the 1945 season weren't monsters. All major schools played some wartime teams, and Alabama fleshed out its own schedule by beating the Army Air Force team of Keesler Field in Mississippi and the Pensacola Naval Air Station squad. But they also beat LSU, South Carolina, Tennessee, and Georgia without breaking much of a sweat, and won the SEC championship with ease.

The 1946 Rose Bowl was never a contest. The Tide players, fueled by the arrogance of the California writers, took a 20–0 halftime lead, cruised to a score of 34–0 at the end of three quarters, and coasted to a 34–13 victory. Like many Alabama bowl victories, it could have been much worse; Coach Frank Thomas, out of respect for Southern Cal coach Jeff Kravaths, cleared his bench with substitutes in the fourth quarter. It was an example of gallantry that Thomas's pupil, Paul Bryant, would often emulate in later years.

Thomas would not say that the '45 team was better than his 1934 unit—a team on which Don Hutson and Bryant had been stars for and which had also been undefeated and a Rose Bowl winner—but he did think that the '45 boys were one of his two best teams.

There was no doubt in Thomas's mind, though, that in 1945 Alabama was the best team in the nation. Army, under Coach Red Blaik, was the true darling of the eastern press, and the cadets walked off with the AP sportswriters' poll and the UPI coaches' poll despite playing only nine games. (One of them against Melville, Long Island's PT boat squad, whom they defeated 55–13.) The United States Military Academy shunned bowl games played during the war years, so the Black Knights of the Hudson stayed home on New Year's Day, rendering Alabama's resounding Rose Bowl win a moot point. The National Championship Foundation, however, felt that both teams were deserving of top honors and voted them co-champions.

The 1962 Crimson Tide was on a nineteen-game winning streak—and twenty-six straight games without a loss—when they found themselves trailing Georgia Tech 7–6 in the fourth quarter. Bear Bryant's sentiments about ties were well known—"like kissing your sister." Alabama opted for the 2-point conversion and failed.

It's interesting to consider what might have happened had Bryant chosen to simply go for the extra point. In 1961 Alabama was, by consensus, the defending national champion, having gone unbeaten the previous year and having outscored eleven opponents by a whopping 272 points. The 1962 squad was very nearly as dominating: despite the loss to Georgia Tech in Atlanta on November 17, the Tide shut out three opponents and had not given up more than a touchdown in the other seven games, largely through the efforts of All-American linebacker Lee Roy Jordan, of whom Bryant said,

"If they stay between the lines, Lee Roy will get them." The 27-point game average on offense, high for its era, reflected the awesome talent of a sophomore quarterback from Beaver Falls, Pennsylvania, named Joe Namath.

For the first eight weeks of the season Alabama led in the major polls, maintaining a slight edge over the USC Trojans, coached by Bryant's friend John McKay. After the Tide lost to Georgia Tech, USC finally got the number-one vote, and Alabama was relegated to second place. In 1962 both the AP and the UPI decided to wait till after the bowl games to vote. The Trojans beat an 8–2 Wisconsin team 42–27 in the Rose Bowl, while in the Orange Bowl, Alabama shut out an 8–2 Oklahoma team coached by the great Bud Wilkinson, 17–0. The Tide's bowl victory was more impressive than the Trojans'. Combined with the aura of being defending champion, it's altogether possible that the Tide could have edged out the Trojans had they preserved their unbeaten record by having settled for a tie against Georgia Tech.

Bryant later insisted he never considered playing for the tie. The College Football Research Center still thought Alabama was a better team than USC and awarded them their version of the national championship.

The 1963 Orange Bowl was the second and final meeting between Bear Bryant and his close friend, Charles Burnham "Bud" Wilkinson. Wilkinson had been a quarterback for Bernard W. "Bernie" Bierman's 1934 Minnesota Golden Gophers, a team that many midwesterners regarded as the equal or superior of the 1934 Alabama Crimson Tide national championship team that Bryant had played on. Wilkinson was fond of chiding Bryant because Alabama was chosen to go to the Rose Bowl that year instead of Minnesota. Some day, he kidded Bryant, they'd settle the issue on the field.

The opportunity came in the 1951 Sugar Bowl when Wilkinson's Sooners, defending national champs and the number-one ranked team for the 1950 season, faced Bryant's Kentucky Wildcats, who had lost just a single game. Though the polls that year closed before the bowl games, everyone knew that a symbolic number-one ranking was at stake; Kentucky won, 13–7, in a colossal upset that established Bryant's national reputation.

In the 1963 Orange Bowl, the Sooners never came close to scoring, which meant in two bowl games Bryant's defense had allowed just seven points against one of the greatest offensive coaches in the history of the game.

For Bryant, the personal confrontation with Wilkinson meant almost as much as the game itself. Bryant made no secret of the fact that he idolized Wilkinson and that the blond, eloquent Bud embodied the image that the truck farmer's son from Arkansas wished he could project. The late Al Browning related that prior to the 1963 Orange Bowl, Bryant was worried that he would come in a sorry second to Wilkinson when they met with President John F. Kennedy, who attended the game. He asked sportswriter Bill Connors to do some spying and find out what Wilkinson was going to be wearing. When Connors couldn't get a straight answer from Bud, Bryant shrugged and said, "I'll just send Mama [his wife, Mary Harmon] down to one of those Palm Beach stores and let her try to guess what kind of Florida clothes Bud would wear." In the Miami heat, though, Wilkinson decided to dress practically, no coat and a white short-sleeved shirt, while Bryant, in a long-sleeved dress shirt, light blue sweater, and new sport coat, sweated uncomfortably for hours. As it turned out, Bryant never got to shake hands with Kennedy on that day.

The president passed up a chance to meet the winning coach in favor of a photo op with Wilkinson. Some suggested that Kennedy was expressing an antipathy toward Alabama's segregated team, but more likely he was courting the Republican Wilkinson, whom he had just appointed head of his Council for Physical Fitness.

For want of 2 points Bear Bryant would not only have won the

1962 national championship, he would have accomplished the incredible feat of winning back-to-back titles twice—1961–1962 and 1964–1965—in the space of five seasons.

If Alabama has a forgotten entry in the WCS sweepstakes, it is the 1975 edition. On September 8 in Birmingham, the Missouri Tigers and their future New York Giants star running back Tony Galbreath stunned the Tide 20–7 in Birmingham. The severity of the loss and the fact that it was a home game for Alabama pretty much erased the Tide from the minds of most voters as a national championship contender. Bryant later admitted that the Monday night starting date, the earliest of his entire career up to that point, had been a mistake—he had been distracted by an impending court case against the National Collegiate Athletic Association, which limited roster sizes.

But from the second week of the season through the bowl games, there was no better team in the country than Alabama. Starting with a 56–0 victory over Clemson on September 20, the Tide thrashed ten consecutive opponents by an aggregate score of 354–46. In the Sugar Bowl on December 31, in the first of four historic meetings between Bear Bryant and Joe Paterno, Bama beat the Penn State Nittany Lions 13–6, with quarterback Richard Todd earning the MVP honors. (It was the first game played in the New Orleans Super Dome.) Bryant would finish with four wins in four tries against the man who would eventually pass him up on the all-time victory list.

Alabama was voted third in the nation behind Oklahoma and Arizona State. More than likely, with a bit more preparation for the opening game, Bryant would have had his second national championship in three years. In a sense, Alabama's near-win in 1975 was the mirror opposite of its near-win in 1974. That year the Tide outscored ten regular season opponents 318–83, defeated Tennessee, LSU, and Auburn 75–19, and lost a heartbreaking Orange Bowl game to Notre Dame 13–11, in which they substantially outgained the Irish. Everyone remembers how close—the length of a chip shot field goal—Alabama came to winning the national championship in 1974.

Because the season's only loss came on the opening day of 1975, relatively few Tide fans look back with regret on that season, during which Alabama convincingly outscored its regular-season opponents 361–66. "I'll tell you this," says Ozzie Newsome, "if they'd have started the season on September 20, we'd have won the national championship no matter who we had to play to do it. From the second game on, we were the best." Herman Matthews, creator of the Matthews Grid Rating, thought so and picked the Tide at number one along with Ohio State, ahead of both the Sooners and the Sun Devils.

Alabama's 1977 team featured some of its all-time great players, including quarterback Jeff Rutledge, running back Tony Nathan, split-end Ozzie Newsome, and defensive back Don McNeal. They lost just one game, by seven points, to the Nebraska Cornhuskers at Lincoln while posting victories over LSU, Tennessee, and Auburn. Their most notable win, though, was over Southern Cal in Los Angeles when Barry Krauss (hero of the next year's immortal goal line stand against Penn State in the Sugar Bowl) intercepted a pass on a 2-point conversion try to preserve Alabama's 21–20 victory.

To Crimson Tide fans (who, we must admit, have a somewhat biased view of the matter) the season ended this way: the Tide went into the bowl games ranked number three with a 10–1 record, whipped Ohio State convincingly, 35–6, in the Sugar Bowl, and *still* wound up number two while the number-five team going into the bowls, Notre Dame, vaulted over them and into the top spot. That is, in fact, what happened, but it does require some background.

The Texas Longhorns, sporting a perfect 11–0 record and paced by their Heisman-Trophy-winning running back, Earl Campbell, were everyone's choice for number one at the end of the regular season. They were double-digit betting favorites against 10–1 number-five-ranked Notre Dame going into the Cotton Bowl. In an amazing turn of events, the bowl games finished like this:

—Notre Dame, coached by Dan Devine and led by junior quarterback Joe Montana, shocked Fred Akers's Longhorns 38–10, eliminating them from the title race. Clearly, the Fighting Irish would move up in the polls; the question was how far would they go?

—In the Orange Bowl, Barry Switzer's number-two-ranked Oklahoma Sooners lost 31–6 to Lou Holtz's 25-point underdog Arkansas Razorbacks. Oklahoma was out.

—Bo Schembechler's Michigan Wolverines had their shot, but were upset by Don James's Washington Huskies 27–20 in the Rose Bowl.

Logically, this left just two teams in contention for the top spot—Alabama and Notre Dame. Both teams had played comparably tough schedules, both teams finished 11–1, and both won their bowl games resoundingly, Alabama by 29 points and Notre Dame by 28. The difference in the eyes of some voters was obviously that Notre Dame had beaten the number-one-ranked team while Alabama had beaten the number-eight-ranked team.

Still, given Alabama's higher ranking before the bowls, there was no good reason why college football couldn't have had two national champions that year—which was exactly what would happen the next year when Alabama and Southern Cal both walked off wearing crowns after the AP and UPI votes. The College Football Research Center, smarter than either AP or UPI, made the Tide and the Irish co-champions for 1977. That's good enough to earn the '77 team another WCS title.

The Sugar Bowl was charged with the excitement generated

by a Bear Bryant-Woody Hayes matchup. Publicly, Bryant played
down the idea of a coaching showdown. Before the game he told
the press, "I don't know why you people keep making such a big
deal over Woody Hayes and Paul Bryant. I assure you I'm not going to play, and I hope Woody does." Privately, said those who were
around him in the weeks before the game, he relished the confrontation.

The game was never in doubt. The Tide drove to the Buckeyes'
three yard line in the first quarter, and Bryant, in an inexplicably
uncharacteristic call, decided to go for a touchdown rather than a
field goal. Ohio State held. It was the only success they would enjoy
all day. Quarterback Jeff Rutledge stretched Ohio State's secondary
with passes to Ozzie Newsome and Bruce Bolton, and Major Ogilvie and Tony Nathan tore through holes on the inside. Afterward,
a smiling Bryant told writers that "Woody is a great coach, and I
ain't bad."

The 1978 Sugar Bowl, by the way, was the only meeting between
the two college coaching titans of the 1950s and 1960s, Paul Bryant and Woody Hayes, who were also the winningest active major
college coaches of their time. Bryant went into the 1978 Sugar Bowl
with 272 victories while Hayes had 231. Woody would win just
seven more games, stepping down at the end of the following season after an embarrassing assault of a Clemson football player on
national television. Bear Bryant, including the historical Sugar
Bowl match, still had 51 career victories to go.

We've taken the 1966 Crimson Tide out of chronological order
and saved it for last because, more than any other Alabama WCS
team—and perhaps more than any other nonchampionship team
in college football history—it has inspired its own legend.

Every Alabama fan knows the story. The Crimson Tide won
back-to-back national championships in 1964 and 1965. By 1966
they were on the verge of history: no college team had ever won

three consecutive national titles. In most other seasons they would have gotten it, but 1966 was different—different from just about any season that had gone before it.

The Tide started slowly, beating Louisiana Tech 34–0 in Birmingham, and then sputtered to a 17–7 victory over Ole Miss in Jackson. Unfortunately for Alabama, two other schools did not start slowly. Duffy Daugherty's Michigan State Spartans had also won a piece of the national championship the year before, placing number one in the UPI coaches' poll, which fortunately for the Spartans, didn't include the bowl games. (MSU lost to UCLA in a major upset in the Rose Bowl.) The Spartans came out roaring in '66, beating North Carolina and Penn State by a combined score of 70–18. Meanwhile, Notre Dame, led back to prominence in 1964 by new coach Ara Parseghian, had defeated Bob Griese and Purdue 26–14 on national television on opening day and followed with a 35–7 win over Northwestern. For the next three weeks, the polls would read: "1. Michigan State, 2. Notre Dame, and 3. Alabama."

That changed on October 15 when Michigan State scraped by Ohio State 11–8 at Columbus. On the same afternoon, Alabama, playing in the rain and mud in its closest call of the year, missed a chance to jump into the top spot when they squeaked by Tennessee 11–10 in Knoxville. Notre Dame beat a weak North Carolina team 32–0 to earn the number-one votes, and the next week routed a strong Oklahoma squad, 38–0, in Norman to widen their lead.

That's the way it went through November when, on the nineteenth, the game everyone had been waiting for since the opening week of the season was played. Notre Dame, playing without starting quarterback Terry Hanratty, who left the field in the first quarter after a hit from the Spartans All-America defensive end, Bubba Smith, fell behind 10–0 then rallied to tie the game. On the final series, Parseghian chose to run the clock out and preserve the tie, assuming that Notre Dame had superior voting clout in the polls. He was right, and after beating Southern Cal 51–0 in

ery Alabama fan was sure that a deserving Crimson Tide was
shafted by voters because of a segregation policy that no longer ap-
plied to student enrollment but was still very much alive on the
football team.

Or, as was often said at the time, "We lost the national championship in '66 because of George Wallace."

Was it true, though? It certainly was true that some sportswriters, who voted in the AP poll, refused to vote for Alabama until the
Tide integrated—Boston area sportswriter Bud Collins once admitted as much to me. And not all of those who didn't vote for Alabama were northerners; the *Los Angeles Times* writer Jim Murray
had been vocal on the issue for years. Even if they had wanted to
vote for Alabama, though, the Tide's big bowl win over Nebraska
would have counted for naught as both AP and UPI had decided to
close their voting that year before the bowl games were played.

Whatever the motivations of the writers, aversion to Alabama's
racial policy doesn't explain why the coaches, among whom Bryant
was enormously popular, didn't vote for the Tide in the UPI poll.
Nor does it explain why three years later an all-white Texas team
was able to win a national championship with the approval of both
sportswriters *and* coaches. Why, then, did Notre Dame edge out
Alabama in 1966?

First, it's easy to forget that it wasn't only Notre Dame but also
Michigan State who finished ahead of the Tide that year. In the
rush to judgment after the ND-MSU game, it was overlooked that

both the Irish *and* the Spartans played for a tie that day. With less than four minutes left to play, Duffy Daugherty chose to have his punter kick the ball away rather than go for it on fourth down— a strange decision in retrospect, as Daugherty—whose team was, after all, ranked number two—was clearly making a statement that he was not going to try to win the game so much as put Notre Dame in a position to lose it. It was also forgotten that Parseghian had called for a pass on the final series against MSU, but his second-string quarterback, Coley O'Brien, was sacked—in the papers the next day, that play went down as a failed rushing attempt. O'Brien, a diabetic, was so weak in the second half of the game he had to be given an insulin shot on the sidelines.

It's true that Bear Bryant would later grumble about what he believed to be the unfairness of the final vote, and he did make some references to Parseghian having settled for a tie—one of his most widely quoted was "We've got a lot of boys going over to Vietnam, and I sure hope they're not going to be playing for a tie." (After Bryant's remark, much was made later of the fact that several Alabama players served in Vietnam, but then, some Notre Dame players did, too, including Rocky Bleier, who won a purple heart and a bronze star in Vietnam and whose exploits later became a book and then a made-for-TV movie under the title *Fighting Back*.)

Many, though, were puzzled that Bryant did not speak up more openly about a college coach settling for a tie. The reasons were probably two-fold. There is, or at least was in the more gentlemanly time, an unwritten rule about coaches openly criticizing other coaches; everyone knew the pressures that coaches faced and that decisions made on the field were worth huge amounts of money to their universities and thus could have a great effect on a coach's job. More to the point, though, was that in his heart, Bryant knew that his good friend and off-season companion, had also played for a tie and that open criticism of Parseghian would invariably come back to bite Daugherty as well.

Second, and the most likely reason Alabama was not voted the championship, is that some voters thought the Irish and the Spartans were better than the Tide. Both played slightly tougher schedules than Alabama, if only because they played each other. Notre Dame averaged 36.2 points per game on offense to Alabama's 26.7, though there's little doubt Bryant could have run up the scores on most of the Tides' opponents. ND actually gave up fewer points than Alabama on defense, 31 to 37. (And one of the TDs allowed by Notre Dame came off an intercepted pass against Purdue.)

Moreover, there is the question of why the entire Notre Dame team should have been punished for what some perceived as a wrong decision by a coach. As Rocky Bleier phrased it to me a few years ago, "I'm not going to blame Coach Parseghian for his decision in that game. I myself would not have played it so cautiously, but I can understand why he did what he did, particularly with Coley [O'Brien] being in such a weakened condition. Late in the fourth quarter I was wide open on the five yard line on a rollout and he threw the ball to the turf three yards in front of me—that's how weak he was. But let me say this: whatever the coach's decision, the team should not be punished because some people didn't agree with it. We should either have been Number One or we shouldn't have, but the vote should not have hinged on a decision the coach made."

Then again, maybe Notre Dame and Michigan State weren't better than Alabama that year. The truth is that all three teams had seasons worthy of national championship honors. It's also true that all three teams are remembered today because of the controversy surrounding that game and the 1966 season, much more so than if any of them had won the title cleanly.

Nineteen sixty-six was one of the pivotal years in college football history. Daugherty's 1965–66 Michigan State crew has never been given the credit it deserved for being one of the first great football teams composed mostly of black athletes, the most prominent of which were the Spartans' enormous tackle (and future star of both the Baltimore Colts and *Police Academy* movies) Bubba Smith and linebacker George Webster, who topped more than one '60s poll as the best defensive college player of the decade. The 1966 Notre Dame-Michigan State game was the most hyped college football game ever played—the press started building it practically in the middle of the season, and it hasn't stopped being discussed or argued to this day. Television ratings for the game were higher than those for the first Super Bowl between the Green Bay Packers and the Kansas City Chiefs less than two months later.

What's amazing in retrospect is that the game wasn't even scheduled for national television. Back then, the NCAA limited each team's exposure to one home game and one away game, and both ND and MSU had had theirs. The network executives gave in to almost overwhelming public pressure and broadcast the game live in the East and on delay in the rest of the country. The decision was the first crack in the NCAA's vise-like grip on the control of college football broadcasts.

This forced many viewers in Alabama to make decisions: Did they want to know the outcome of the Notre Dame-Michigan State *before* watching it? Or did they want to watch the delayed broadcast and hope for the tie that seemed to be Alabama's only hope to move into the top spot. My family was in transit from the Northeast the day before the game. On Saturday afternoon, driving past Atlanta, we listened to the game on the Mutual Network, which broadcast the Notre Dame games nationwide. Just as we pulled into Birmingham, Notre Dame missed its attempt at a winning field goal. Unaware of the tape delay, I ran across the street to the home of a neighbor, Charlie Reagan, who (though an Auburn fan) had been waiting all month for the game, and proclaimed, "Mr. Reagan, you'll never believe what happened! They tied!" "Allen!" he exclaimed. "Now why did you have to go and ruin that for me?!" To my astonishment, Notre Dame and Michigan State had just kicked off on TV.

The polls, too, were changed by the titanic struggle among the

Irish, the Spartans, and the Crimson Tide for the national championship. The 1966 season marked the last time that they would vote on a national championship *before* the bowl games, and this in turn had the effect of forcing the University of Notre Dame to rethink its policy of shunning postseason games. (Within three years the Fighting Irish would accept an invitation to play number-one-ranked Texas in the Cotton Bowl.) It also caused the Big Ten to rethink its bowl policy; within a few years the conference not only lifted its restriction on having a team go to the Rose Bowl two years in a row, it also began allowing teams other than its champion to go to any bowl they were invited to. Nineteen sixty-six was the last year the championship of college football would be decided on a *college* football field; after that, the final rankings would be determined by the outcomes of bowl games.

From the viewpoint of Alabama fans, the 1966 season was just as momentous. The resentment over going 11–0 then finishing no higher than third in the final polls stirred much debate about the integration of the Alabama football team. It probably wasn't true that segregation kept Alabama from winning an unprecedented third straight national title in 1966, but the fact that many thought it did forced a great many people to think about the future. Within three years, Bryant—who had been working toward integration since 1959, when he took his team to the Liberty Bowl and faced an integrated Penn State team—offered the school's first grant-in-aid to a black player, Wilbur Jackson. If losing the national championship in 1966 was the price Bear Bryant paid for facilitating the integration of the Crimson Tide, who could look back on the teams of the 1970s and argue that the price wasn't worth it?

Let's give 1966 Notre Dame, Michigan State, and Alabama each a WCS championship and call it even for all time.

# Contributors

ERYK ANDERS played at Alabama from 2006–09 as a linebacker. The San Antonio, Texas, native made ninety-eight career tackles, including nineteen tackles for loss with eight and a half sacks. He started for two seasons with the Crimson Tide. He made one of the key plays in Alabama's victory over Texas for the Bowl Championship Series national title at the Rose Bowl in Pasadena, California, forcing a fumble on a sack with the Crimson Tide up just three points with a little more than three minutes remaining on the clock. Alabama recovered and converted the turnover into a touchdown to take command of the game. Anders remained in athletics, but not in football. He is pursuing a career as a professional mixed martial arts fighter, based out of Birmingham.

JAVIER ARENAS played at Alabama from 2006–2009, making his mark in the record books as a punt and kickoff returner while also developing to become a standout defensive back. The native of Tampa, Florida, finished as the Crimson Tide's all-time leader in kickoff return yards (2,166) and punt return yards (1,752), finishing just nine yards short of Wes Welker's NCAA record for career punt return yards. He earned All-America and All-SEC honors in 2009 as a senior and was SEC Special Teams Player of the Year. A second-round draft choice by the Kansas City Chiefs, he played from 2010–14 in the pro league and was on the roster of five different teams.

WAYNE ATCHESON served for twenty-two years in The University of Alabama athletic department, including three national football championships in 1964, 1965, and 1992. He was a graduate assistant in sports publicity in 1964–66, sports information director from 1983 to 1987 and associate director of Tide Pride until 2003. He served as secretary of the Paul Bryant Museum Committee until its opening from 1983 to 1988. He has written five books, including *In Due Time* (the Jay Barker story) and *Faith of the Crimson Tide*. Today, Wayne is director of the Billy Graham Library in Charlotte, North Carolina.

ALLEN BARRA has been a columnist and feature writer for the *Wall Street Journal* since 1995. He is also a columnist for the *Village Voice* and a frequent contributor to the *New York Sun*, the *New York Times*, the *Los Angeles Times*, and the *Washington Post Book World*. He is the author of *The Last Coach: A Life of Paul "Bear" Bryant* and *Clearing the Bases: The Greatest Baseball Debates of the Century*, a *Sports Illustrated* Book of the Year. Barra is a graduate of Mountain Brook High School and The University of Alabama in Birmingham. His first Alabama game was in 1966 at Legion Field when Alabama beat Auburn 31–0.

BILL BATTLE has a long connection with The University of Alabama, which began when he enrolled at the Capstone as a biology major and a member of the Crimson Tide football team. When he left he had a master's degree in education, three football letters, and was part of the 1961 national championship team under legendary coach Paul Bryant. Later he became head football coach for the University of Tennessee. He had a very successful business career and was a generous donor to the school. In 2013 he returned to the Alabama campus as athletic director, serving until 2017. Today he is a special assistant to the president of the university and is a member of the Alabama Sports Hall of Fame. He was the 2005 recipient of the Paul W. Bryant Alumni-Athlete Award.

JOHN DAVID BRILEY is an associate professor of political science at East Tennessee State University. He studied at The University of Alabama, Middle Tennessee State University, and the University of Tennessee. Briley served under Paul W. Bryant during the 1973 season as a student athletic trainer. He was a contributor to *Champions in Crimson* (1998), *The Last Coach* (2005) by Allen Barra, *Turning of the Tide* (2006) by Don Yaeger, and *Bear's Boys* (2007) by Eli Gold and M. B. Roberts. Briley is the author of *Career in Crisis: Paul "Bear" Bryant and the 1971 Season of Change* (2006). He lives in Morristown, Tennessee, with his wife, Susan.

TOMMY DEAS has been with the *Tuscaloosa News* since 1993, covering University of Alabama athletics, including football. He was promoted to executive sports editor in 2008 and was named president of the Associated Press Sports Editors in 2016.

MITCH DOBBS was the assistant editor of *'BAMA Magazine* and BamaMag.com from 2004 to 2007. Dobbs worked in The University of Alabama's athletics media relations department from 2003 to 2004 with the football, baseball, and tennis teams, and as an undergraduate student assistant from 1999 to 2002. Dobbs graduated from The University of Alabama's College of Commerce and Business Administration in 2002 and earned a master's degree in marketing from the UA in 2006. Dobbs has done freelance work for various print, radio, and television media, including authoring the screenplay for the *Crimson Classics* television/DVD series "3rd Saturday Glory," "Shula to Bell to Victory," and the 1993 Sugar Bowl episodes. Mitch has worked as an attorney and is currently serving our country as a diplomat.

ANDREW DOYLE is associate professor of history at Winthrop University. He now lives in Rock Hill, South Carolina, with his wife, Rita, who, like him, grew up in Alabama knowing that Bear Bryant was the best there ever was. He has published a number of journal articles on the social and cultural history of early southern football and is now finishing a book manuscript on that subject.

KEITH DUNNAVANT is the author of several books, including biographies of Paul "Bear" Bryant, Bart Starr and Joe Montana, as well as *The Missing Ring*, which focuses on the 1966 Alabama football team's pursuit of perfection in an imperfect world. Dunnavant started covering the SEC as a teenager and became a national college football writer for *The National Sports Daily* before moving into magazine management and ownership. His expertise on football history has been featured on ESPN, HBO, and Showtime. *Three Days at Foster*, his documentary film about the pioneer African-American athletes who shattered the UA color barrier, is available on Amazon.

KENNETH GADDY is a native of Thomasville, Alabama, and a graduate of the University of South Alabama. He served as curator of the Alabama Museum of Natural History for four years, where he led the summer Museum Expedition program in addition to managing the collections. Gaddy joined the staff of the Paul W. Bryant Museum in 1991, later becoming director. He has been the executive producer for the museum's *Crimson Classics* and *Crimson Comments* television series. Gaddy is married to Scarlett, and they have one son, Michael.

WINSTON GROOM is a 1965 graduate of The University of Alabama. After serving in Vietnam as a lieutenant with the Fourth Infantry Division, he became a journalist in Washington until 1977, when he left to write his first novel, *Better Times Than These*, about the war. He has written many books, including *Forrest Gump, Conversations with the Enemy*, which was nominated for the Pulitzer Prize, and *The Crimson Tide: An Illustrated History of Football at The University of Alabama*. He lives with his wife and family in Point Clear, Alabama.

BARRETT JONES finished his Alabama career as perhaps the most decorated player in the program's rich history. Jones, who started fifty games on the offensive line, played guard, center, and tackle. He redshirted in 2008 and played from 2009–12 as part of three national championship and two SEC title teams. The Memphis native won the Outland Trophy, the Rimington Trophy, the Jacobs Blocking Trophy, the Wuerffel Trophy, and the William V. Campbell Trophy, known as college football's "Academic Heisman." Jones's father, Rex, played basketball at Alabama in the 1980s, and his brothers Harrison and Walker both played football at the Capstone.

WALT MADDOX is serving his fourth term as mayor of Tuscaloosa. Mayor Maddox is nationally recognized for his crisis management following the tornado that struck Tuscaloosa on April 27, 2011. He was named municipal Leader of the Year as he led the city's recovery efforts, demonstrating his strong, decisive, and comforting leadership. Maddox has a Political Science undergraduate degree and Public Administration graduate degree from the University of Alabama in Birmingham, and he lettered four years on the football team. He is an avid runner and created an annual race to benefit pre-K education in Tuscaloosa.

KIRK MCNAIR, founder and editor of *'Bama: Inside the Crimson Tide* and BamaMag.com and the author of *What It Means to Be*

*Crimson Tide*, was Alabama sports information director in 1978. He is past president of the National Collegiate Sports Publications and the Alabama Sports Writers Associations. He has written and edited numerous articles on Alabama football and won national writing awards. The Birmingham native is a graduate of Maryville College and has taken graduate writing courses at Alabama. He and his wife, Lynne, married since 1963, have children Julia, a graduate of Vanderbilt, and Stuart, a graduate of Texas A&M, and grandchildren Roeder Kirk McNair, Jordan Elisabeth McNair, and Henry Kirk Allsup.

DELBERT REED is an award-winning journalist and author who has won first-place writing awards in Alabama and Mississippi and first- and second-place national writing awards. His work has appeared in numerous regional and national publications. Reed, a former sports editor of *The Tuscaloosa News*, holds BS and MA degrees from The University of Alabama and is the author of *Paul "Bear" Bryant: What Made Him a Winner*, *When Winning Was Everything*, *All of Us Fought the War*, *Mike Denny: The Shadow of a Single Man*, and *Delbert Reed & Friends*, a collection of his favorite newspaper columns.

TOM ROBERTS grew up in Fayette, Alabama, where he started his broadcasting career at WWWF. He attended The University of Alabama, working as sports editor of the *Crimson White*. He served as news director and sports director at Tuscaloosa radio stations WNPT and WTBC. In 1972, Roberts moved to Birmingham to join WVTM-TV. He stayed there nineteen years as a news and sports anchor, the last eight years as news director. Tom was part of the Crimson Tide Sports Network from 1978 until his retirement in 2015. He produced the Nick Saban TV show and the Mark Gottfried TV show. He hosted Sarah Patterson's television show. Tom was the host of the network's football broadcasts and the weekly coaches call-in show, "Hey Coach." Tom has two sons, Elliott and Brian.

PHIL SAVAGE has served as the color analyst for the Crimson Tide Sports Network since 2009 and is also the Executive Director of the Reese's Senior Bowl in Mobile. After receiving a Bachelor's Degree in English from the University of the South in 1987, he embarked on a twenty-five-year coaching and scouting career that began at The University of Alabama and included stints with UCLA (1991), the Cleveland Browns (1991–1995), the Baltimore Ravens (1996–2004), the Browns again as General Manager (2005–2008), and the Philadelphia Eagles (2010–2012).

GENE STALLINGS, now retired, lives with his wife, Ruth Ann, on a ranch in his hometown of Paris, Texas. Stallings played for Coach Paul W. Bryant at Texas A&M from 1954 to 1956, enduring the now legendary Junction City training camp in 1954. Stallings served as a student assistant coach with the Aggies in 1957 before following Bryant to Alabama in 1958. After seven years on Bryant's staff, Stallings left Tuscaloosa in 1965 to become the head coach at his alma mater where he remained until 1971. He served on Tom Landry's staff with the Dallas Cowboys from 1972 to 1985 and then spent four years as the head coach of the St. Louis/Phoenix Cardinals. Stallings returned to Alabama in 1990, this time as head coach, and guided the Crimson Tide to the 1992 national championship. He retired in 1996.

ERIK STINNETT, a Tuscaloosa native, has served as a regular contributor to 'BAMA Magazine since 2004. In 2005, he assisted Kirk McNair with the book, *What It Means to Be Crimson Tide*, and in 2006 he wrote the script for "Chasing History and a Hound," part of Bryant Museum's *Crimson Classics* series. Prior to that, Stinnett worked six years as a sportswriter.

STEVE TOWNSEND is the author of four books on Crimson Tide football: *Season of Champions, Talk of the Tide: An Oral History of Alabama Football, Crimson Heart,* and *A Time of Champions: Tales from the 1978–79 Alabama Football Seasons.* He served in a number of roles at the university since beginning his career as the associate commissioner of the Southeastern Conference. While serving as associate athletic director at UA, Townsend also served as the cochairman of the 1992 Centennial Celebration. During his tenure at the SEC, he initiated the Football Media Week, was the media coordinator of the Sugar Bowl, and worked as a media liaison at five Final Fours. He won twenty-two national awards for his publications at the SEC and the university.

TAYLOR WATSON is curator of the Paul W. Bryant Museum and the producer of the award-winning television series *Crimson Classics* and *Crimson Comments,* and is the author of *Inside the Vault: The Paul W. Bryant Collection.* He has served the Paul W. Bryant Museum for twenty-five years, and during that period has assisted with over one hundred book, video, radio, and motion picture projects. The Huntsville native is a graduate of The University of Alabama. He and his wife, Barbara, have been together since 1986 and have two children, Amber and Keya.